Quality Mind
Quality Life

To Ellen & Joe:
I am so happy for knowing
you both — you are truly
Quality people —
I extend my every wish
for your happiness and our
continued friendship —
Love —
Carl
Lisnet

Quality Mind

Quality Life

by
Paul M. Lisnek

Dedication

... for my parents, Seymour and Sandy Lisnek. You are my guiding
light and beacon of my every hope

Acknowledgements

The basis of this book is the pursuit of quality—in our minds and our lives. The fundamental component of quality can be found in the people who are our resources, our spirit, our support, and our salvation. As you read this book, you should know that I have been guided and supported by some special people, without whom this book would not exist. They insured that this labor remained a labor of love and hope.

No stronger love and guidance could be extended to me than that of my parents, Seymour and Sandy Lisnek. And so I return, if only through this small dose, my deepest love and respect. You are the lifeblood and quality in my work and success. Thanks also to my brother Rick and his beloved wife Judy, my nephews David and Michael and niece Danielle, all of who provide never-ending support and encouragement. To Dave Jorbin and to the memory of Dalcy, remember that I shall forever appreciate your pride in my efforts.

Special thanks to my professional support team in the office: Craig Balmer, Anne Brody, Richard Anton, Dave Johnson, "Sam the Man," and Diana Briggs. You keep me running and meeting the obligations! And thanks to Bob Sandidge for recognizing the fit with Meta Publications and for being the Creative Core of this operation.

No more professional appreciation can be more important than that which I extend to the prolific Virginia McCullough. For your guidance throughout this project, input in its design and structure, feedback on the writing and style, and suggested alterations when the concepts might have been made more clear, you are single-handedly responsible for insuring that this book has seen the light of day. You have stayed with me and this project from its inception, and now we shall together see the offspring that these long hard efforts have produced—I thank you, I thank you!

To Chris and Anthony Salamone, my partners in the quality program, the National Institute for Legal Education, our efforts to insure that future lawyers and professionals receive the best preparatory education possible. You and the institute are the best examples of the quality mind/quality life concepts this book seeks to teach.

To Julie Eichorn, thanks for always believing in me and supporting my efforts to reach for the sky.

I extend special thanks to Richard Gabriel and Jo-Ellan Dimitrius for making me a part of their quality trial consulting team and for the quality they bring to their clients, the attorneys in such cases as the Rodney King/LAPD case, Reginald Denny, Heidi Fleiss, and O. J. Simpson. Who knows what important cases the future shall bring?

To the Reverend Arnold Pierson, a friend confidant of many years, thanks for supporting me in the tough times and knowing that a rainbow always awaited beyond the rain.

And thanks to those who permit me the privilege of enjoying our deep and ever-growing friendships, with my hope that we all continue to seek and strive for total quality in our professional and personal lives: Steve Pearson, Raymond Massey, Michael Mendelson, Cindy Raymond, Larry Bushong, Barry Litwin, Bob Anderson, Marcia Moulton, Michael Menefee, Al Menotti, Mimi Mouakad, Robert Bell, Steve and Hester Rubin, Marlene Rubin, Ken and Tricia Fischbein, Emilio and Leslie Machado, Byron McCoy, Tony and Cathy Parrilli, Edie Reese-Gordon, Alvina Norman, Steve Friedland, Steve Coffman, Cathie Kopecky, Sarkis Yoghourdjian, Jim Rogner, Ron

Acknowledgements

Matlon, Mark Buhrke, Ben and Georgia Haglund, Steve Gan, David Greengus, Joseph Cisneros, Andy Perez, Mary and Dick Murphy, and Jerry and Dottie Fugiel-Smith. May others be as fortunate as I am in having and enjoying such relationships.

Finally, thanks to my NBC News colleagues, Arthur Lord and Claude Novak, for their good humor and personal encouragement.

And to you, the reader, who has already made a commitment to bring quality into your life. I offer my most sincere appreciation for your trust that this book can be your starting point and guide to committing yourself to a mind and life of quality.

Enjoy the journey.

Paul M. Lisnek
June, 1995

Chapter I

The Premise and the Promise

---

66 THE GRASS IS ALWAYS GREENER on the other side of the fence," some people say, as they continue to sit out the opportunities for personal growth and balance in their lives.

"Other people always seem to be able to work through their problems," one friend says to another, "but I just stay stuck in mine."

"While other people grab for the brass ring, I'm always willing to settle for just enough," the great multitudes say, either out loud or to themselves.

These comments are so common that we often overlook the fact that the words are incredibly self-defeating. But, we hear these kinds of self-disparaging remarks in every part of this country and from people across a variety of professions, races, and personality types. These self-deprecating statements are actually calls for help from people who truly want to develop and improve their professional or personal lives—or strive to balance the two—but don't know how to get there. The task isn't easy.

It isn't so surprising that many people come to believe that *other* people have their lives all put together—everyone except themselves. These endless comparisons with others who seem to be "making it" lead them to believe that they are coming up short. They just don't seem to get it together like other people do, no matter how hard they try. The unfortunate result is that too many people wind up seeing and judging themselves as "might-have-beens." What a waste of talent and life energy.

The truth is that we are all on the search for the brass ring—we are all in the process of going after it. The good news is, the ring is within reach and may be closer than you think. You may not be able to see it, or even sense it, because you are too busy comparing yourself to others. It's time to step out of the struggle and into a new milieu.

The distress caused by the internal struggle we feel when life seems to pass us by leads millions of people on a search for answers. You picked up this book, so I conclude you are one of the activists, one of the seekers. If you are a corporate employee, you may frequently scan up and down the business shelves in bookstores as you look for a sophisticated tome that will provide the answers to your professional life.

Perhaps you glance through countless self-help books looking for motivation, healing, or a path to inner peace. Each book seems to provide a good idea or two, but you are left with incomplete answers, a sense that there must be something else out there that can help.

Not long ago, I was struck with an idea, similar to an "ah ha," experience, that a more complete answer to so many of life's dilemmas must lie in a convergence of the worlds of business and self-help. What if we combined the best of what the business arena has to offer with the most insightful of the guides to probe and improve the inner self? This book is the result of my work to merge the best of two of the most important movements of our era.

Although it may not be obvious at first glance, this merger is nothing short of revolutionary because both fields offer such a powerful body of knowledge. The personal growth, self help, or human potential movements have affected every aspect of life in our country—some say the entire world. There is immense energy in the information we can glean from our search of the inner self to find our own personal answers to difficult life problems. Perhaps the reason that this energy seems to come and go in spurts and gasps is that we haven't known how to effectively channel it.

People who succeed in an endeavor to uncover their great potential in career or personal life need a strong inclination—and the freedom—to explore their own lives, set goals, and actually reach them. A spark of motivation must come first, and millions of people have shown that they are quite willing to accept this challenge. They demonstrate that they yearn to participate in the world in a richer and deeper way than ever before as they attend seminars, read books, join study groups, and so forth.

However, as we all know, many of us stop short of taking the steps necessary to actually implement the phases of change—the very change we say we want. Perhaps we can blame it on the limitations of human nature, but sometimes the changes that need to be made to achieve success may seem too difficult to try, too distant to reach. Perhaps the spirit isn't willing, or maybe the dedication to succeed just isn't as strong as the person suspected. However, with the right ingredients, change can be irresistible, inviting, and welcomed. That's what this book provides—the ingredients needed to follow a recipe for success.

"But," you say, "I keep trying to implement changes, but I end up feeling trapped." Indeed, there are always perceived traps, many of which can be understood when we look at where we were born and how our parents lived their lives. And we find that it's easy to follow their lead, and ultimately, to get trapped in the patterns of the past. Since our models are our families, the models are comfortable and we assume that their direction is one we should follow too—especially if they worked hard to clear a path for us.

As Americans, we have long been proud that, largely because of our vast resources, so many of us have been able to break new ground. Many of our parents broke new ground for their generations, but we must be careful not to take their example too literally. Part of our nation's rich tradition is taking advantage of the freedom to develop skills and directions for our lives.

Our task is to change those teachings of the past that can be improved upon. This means questioning the status quo—realizing that each of us is a combination of strengths and imperfections. Growth comes from challenging ourselves to improve and not from saying, "Oh well, this is who I am and there is no way I can change." Far from it, we can move our lives towards perfection, faults and all.

Perfection: Faults and All

Consider a paradox. We are an imperfect society, but we are all perfect people. As a group, we can start wars, lose business, and work together in an unending quest for creative solutions to our problems. (You know the old adage: a camel is a horse designed by committee). Yet the perfection of each individual is a fundamental concept which underlies this book. I ask you to assume that people are created perfect—and that includes you.

This isn't a difficult concept once you think about it. You might wonder how we can be perfect if we often mess up a task or crash a project. Sometimes our mess-ups are of relatively little importance, but at other times, we can reel for weeks or years over them.

Even when you mess up a situation, you mess it up perfectly. In fact, you doubt if anyone could have messed it up as well as you did. Agree? Then accept that with each fault, each mistake, and each skill, you are a perfect specimen of a human being. You can learn to deal with your shortcomings and can learn to see each failure as a mechanism for feedback. In this way, you learn constantly how *not* to do things and try again to find the proper way that will lead to an answer.

Look at it this way: when an actor needs twelve takes to get a scene right, each take was an exercise in perfection—each perfect mess-up provided the information to get it right. No one could have messed up as well as this actor; no one could fix it as well either. So you're given a project at work and get yelled at because it wasn't completed exactly the way your supervisor expected it to be done. Is this your fault? It depends on who you ask.

The important point is to learn where your work failed to match the supervisor's expectations. This is the realm in which learning occurs. Perhaps you need to ask more questions before undertaking a project for that person, or perhaps that person needs to provide additional information—once it becomes clear that clarity is lacking.

In relationships, we often find ourselves at odds with someone we love. We usually don't mean to act on misunderstanding, but sometimes we just don't create an overlap between our actions and what the other person expects of us. Did you buy the wrong birthday gift? Maybe you showed up late for a date, but only because you wanted to pick up a gift for that special person? As always, no one can mess up as well as we can, but these are the moments for learning. These are the times we learn how things should be done. What better way is there to learn than by the responses you get when you don't do what someone else expected you to do?

Learn and Take Charge

It's important to believe that now, more than ever before, we have the capacity to write our own life agendas and to take control of our own destinies. The key to succeeding at this self-direction is to uncover the available resources each of us has within us. Then we must learn how to locate and channel other important resources we need to achieve professional and personal success. We must then integrate them into our increasing inventory of strengths and skills.

Why should any of this matter? Why should we bother? The answer is as close as the daily newspaper. Does a day go by that we do not read about lay-offs, jobs that travel south of the border or across the Pacific, mergers, hostile take-overs, and so on? People who once believed their jobs were secure find themselves standing in the unemployment line. I suspect that most of us know someone—or we are that someone—who is looking for a new job. Ironically, this bad news was the impetus for this book. It was this bad news that told me to synthesize a new and better way to make our way through the world.

It's in these difficult times that a shake-up in your approach might lead you to seek something stronger, something better, to shape your future. I'm not sure that there has ever been a time in history that wasn't described by those living in it as "difficult." Still, for the sake of simplicity, let's assume that our era is especially chaotic because of the rapidity of the change we are experiencing.

The challenge of change lies first in recognizing that a new path is necessary, and second in having the guts to act and implement the changes we discover are essential. The way in which the recognition of this need and the actions that follow are handled will determine whether the outcome of our change is vigorous growth or empty stagnation.

One of the most fundamental and exciting elements of this age of personal growth is the belief that people have, within themselves, the ability to uncover an answer to just about any problem that confronts them. Take a minute and consider what resources already exist in our world: support groups to help us recover from illnesses and addictions; therapeutic systems that help us solve problems; and still other programs which invite participants to actively explore ways to expand their minds. Some people believe that we are only beginning to tap into the enormous potential of the human brain.

Each of these tools teaches us that positive growth is almost always accompanied by the pain of revelation and change. The pain isn't pleasant, but it isn't negative either—it's the sure sign that we can change. After all, it is usually pain that triggers the need to seek answers in the first place.

Complacency, by its very nature, rarely leads anyone to seek help or create change. So, if you are reading this book and are already considering the ideas discussed here, then you are likely experiencing some unpleasantness in your life—at least to some degree. Maybe you perceive that change is needed, even if you can't explain why or know what area of your life needs some examination. Or, change may be forced upon you because you have lost your job or a relationship has ended. Perhaps you simply desire to reject or break away from the status quo because it feels like shoes that are pinching your feet. No matter what the motive, each of us can effect some change in our lives.

As I talk to people during my lectures and seminars across this country, I'm constantly astounded by how many people are on an active search for a plan or system that can change their lives. Most of us realize that while the ultimate answers are within us, we can benefit from the guidance and expertise that others have to offer. It's true that some people want the blueprint laid out in front of them; some even want others to do all the work. This is impossible. We have to do the footwork ourselves in order to get the real rewards. However, we can use the vast resources available.

This book will teach you how to find all the answers you need; it will guide you as you search within *yourself*. Of course, you will need assistance from others and you will need resources outside of those you already have. And you'll learn how to go about assessing what you need and what you can ask of others.

This book will teach you that figuring out what is missing from your personal formula for success and happiness is a relatively simple task. It involves pulling together what you need after recognizing the pain you are experiencing right now. You will then sense your strong desire to seek an answer. And finally, you will gather and channel all the resources necessary to implement the plan you will devise for your life.

One thing will become abundantly clear: You are capable of great achievement, success, and happiness when you choose to take control of your own destiny. If you are reading this book, you have likely already made a choice to expand and put into effect a system that urges you toward growth. My goal for this book is helping you gain the *practical* tools to work with in your own personal pursuit of happiness. Only then, can your ongoing search in the outside world come to settle in the comfort of the answers that lie inside you.

Getting Down to Business

The promises of personal growth I am making here are sincere. They emerge, not from the world of self-help literature alone, but rather, the promises are grounded in the sophisticated—and often shrewd—world of business. While the business community has recently experienced upheavals and economic downturn, it is also indisputable that some of the brightest and most insightful minds in the country work in that arena. If we can tap into the best of the business world and integrate it with a personal success component, then we have the formula for unlimited success. We are limited only by our imagination.

The key to growth in the business community in the 1990s may be already familiar to you, at least by its name, the *quality movement*. Perhaps you've already been touched by this movement, because in varying degrees it has become part of most workplaces, both large and small. In a word, the quality movement has done for the business community what the personal growth revolution has accomplished for individuals who have sought and implemented its many messages. Welcome to their merger in the ultimate personal quality success program.

In business, the revolution is well known as Total Quality Management (TQM) or Total Quality Control (TQC). The "quality" movement has been labeled, dissected, and discussed in many ways in the business world. Whether we call it TQM, TQC or simply a commitment to quality, the essence of this movement is an attempt to change attitudes about what is *possible*. W. Edwards Deming, Philip Crosby, and Joseph Juran have become household names—or perhaps more appropriately, boardroom, factory, and office names. For decades, these leaders have been influencing work environments all over the world. In fact, America's primary economic competitor, Japan, credits Deming and Juran for helping to build their country into the international economic giant it has become. After World War II, W. Edwards Deming was hired as a consultant by the Japanese to assist them in a monumental task, rebuilding their industries—indeed, rebuilding their entire country. In Japan, say the name Deming, and people think "quality."

Oddly enough, interest in this particular type of quality movement didn't begin in earnest in this country until we found ourselves losing our competitive edge in the global economic climate. Paradoxically, this makes sense since, as I've indicated, change doesn't come about without some pain. In the United States, our economic pain was intensified as we noticed Japan growing and prospering as we stagnated and declined. It was a reality that moved business leaders to react and act.

Some people, those who have not thought out the issue very well, resorted to the easy and reactive route—they simply began to "bash" Japan. This ugly reaction was defensive and unproductive, and most serious leaders within the American business community renewed their commitment to rebuilding this country's economic life, rather than indulge in bashing. These forward-thinking leaders chose to *act*, not merely react in an irrational way. They began to adopt the TQM model in industries that have experienced decline and the new high-tech companies that have carried our economy in recent years.

It is these quality elements of the quality movement that yearn to be integrated within the personal growth movement. I began to ask the questions that eventually led to the concepts explained in this book. If quality can be the key to economic prosperity (and it is proving to be just that), then why can't the relevant concepts be integrated into our personal lives? If we think about quality in relation to products and services, then why can't we apply the word to the way we live, work, love, and play? The result would certainly be personal prosperity and renewed energy and vigor in our culture.

Companies are jumping on the quality bandwagon so fast that no one has been able to keep track of the impact the movement has had. One after another, businesses are realizing that they will have a bleak future if they do not recognize that the old ways of producing and managing will put them out of business. This revolution is not restricted to manufacturing. Service industries and retailers—we will all be glad to know—are currently embracing this quality wave.

Those who will succeed are planning their futures around the drive for quality. It's safe to say that whatever field you happen to be in, it will soon be influenced by the TQM movement. The time seems ripe to integrate the concepts into our own lives, thereby gaining maximum control over our destinies.

Sounds good? So what's the problem? Why hasn't this been done before? The answer is both simple and disappointing. You see, one would imagine that upon hearing about quality, few would hesitate to jump in and learn. However, logical as that might seem, the reality is that human beings are resistant to change. Yes, business and other institutions are slow to change and adapt, but most individuals don't lag too far behind in their reluctance to change. For example, in my own field, law, and in many corporate environments in which I consult, I see many lawyers and professionals who remain convinced that an excellent work product is the only measure of their professionalism and ultimately, of their success. Furthermore, they believe that as long as they keep producing good results, clients will be plentiful.

My colleagues, with all due respect, are sadly mistaken. More than anything else, clients demand service, service, service, but some providers aren't willing to comply. They stick to the existing standards of service, whatever they are and however low they may be. Recently, I served as moderator for a panel discussion sponsored by a major law firm in Chicago. The panel consisted of the firm's clients and the audience was the firm's lawyers. The lawyers were transfixed as they listened to their clients discuss why they sent business to their firm. The clients repeatedly centered their comments around service. There was nary a peep about winning or losing cases—service was what was on their minds.

Finally, a lawyer in the audience asked if the quality of the work mattered at all. He was clearly mystified by what he was hearing. One long-standing entrepreneurial client of the firm had a good answer for him. "Of course it matters," he said. "Show me a good loser and I'll show you a loser. But excellent work and skill are *assumed*— without them I wouldn't be here talking to you. If you want to *keep* my business, though, then you better continue making efforts to know *who* I am and what my business is all about. I'm demanding more than good work—I want service—quality service." This client had changed his standards and he was challenging the firm to join him. He had his finger on the pulse of the business climate.

It makes perfect sense that on a personal level, the requirements and responsibilities of our lives also demand service, service, service. Our boss wants our time; our family wants our time; friends, colleagues, and acquaintances all "need" our attention and service. We are often unable or unwilling to meet these demands. Is our personal reaction similar to the lagging corporate response? I say yes. In fact, I suggest that individual responses are trapped between the precedent of the past and the experiences of the present. We know that we must adapt, but we aren't quite sure how.

Don't we owe dedication to ourselves in work and in personal relationships? This book proposes what is both revolutionary, and at the same time, so simple that its absence in our lives is ludicrous: I say that we must uncover the full service quality in ourselves and bring it into every component of our lives. The result will be overall quality, success, and happiness at work, in relationships, and with ourselves.

Excellence in work product and skill is often assumed by business clients, and perhaps by us in our own lives as well. Most of us have been educated to think in terms of skills and ability and, of course, the results we achieve. If we did the actual job well, we assumed that we had it made. Perhaps that's why many of us haven't thought much about service; we haven't evaluated either how we receive or give service in our own lives. But if we wish to succeed, we must learn the requirements or expectations others have for us, including those that reach beyond work product. Similarly, we need to demand, from others and ourselves, more than good work. We owe ourselves and others service—quality service.

There isn't anything inherently wrong with expecting and producing excellence in what we do either at work or in our relationships. But, as the law firm's client pointed out, an excellent "product" is assumed these days. Today's quality is defined in terms of service.

Linking Worlds: Business and Personal

Perhaps you are already sensing the importance and value of integrating the worlds of personal growth with the concepts of the quality movement in business. These movements need to be linked, and in more ways than may be obvious at first glance. The more I've examined the underlying ideas of these important revolutions, the more I realize that when put together, their collective ability to empower each of us is astounding. Their combined ability to empower is more astounding than either movement's individual influence in its own arena.

Cindy, a friend of mine, went to a seminar with the expectation of finding her way out of a rut she had fallen into. More than anything else, I imagine, she went to the seminar infused with a sense of hope. She anticipated that by the end of the day, she would create a set of goals and a plan to reach them. In fact, the seminar leader promised as much.

"The leader talked about vision," Cindy reported to me. "He made me realize that I've been living my life without a real vision of what I want to do, what my deepest desires are, or where I want to be in five or ten years—much less six months from now. Hey, I figured that I could see where I wanted to end up in the future and then lock into that image. Unfortunately, I was stunted by the fear that I might not achieve those goals, and I have yet to take *any* step towards change at all!"

What was the use of Cindy making the effort to learn the means for change if she couldn't take the necessary steps towards its achievement? As if prophetically, I talked just a few weeks later to a man named Ted, who owns a small service business employing 15 people. Business wasn't good for him, a fact that he had blamed on the never-ending recession, his employees' lack of enthusiasm, and ever-increasing taxes.

Ted came to me for some advice on how he might claw his way out of his business doldrums. I asked him a simple question, "Where do you want this business to be in five years?" Ted tried to joke away the truth by responding that he just hoped his business would still exist by the middle of next year. "Well," I said, "if that's all you want, that's probably all you'll get. Before you do anything to change things around here, you better come up with a vision. Forget the plan for now, just create a vision for yourself and your business."

This direct and honest statement startled Ted into seeing the obvious. Ted went on to say that he was afraid to make changes because he worried that he wouldn't like the results. Like Cindy, Ted was just treading the waters of the status quo.

Self-help seminar leaders and business consultants often give the same basic advice to a variety of people who seek revelations, face moments of truth, and wrestle with hard facts. In my travels around the country, I listen carefully to people and the concerns they share with me and with each other. I note again and again what they ultimately come to realize as true: "If my life is going to change, I'm the one that's going to have to do it."

How right these people are. But first, these people need a handle on a vision that can guide them and the guts to take the first step towards their vision. They need to see the chance to create change as an opportunity, not as an obstacle; taking steps toward growth needs to be moments filled with enthusiasm, not trepidation.

Getting Full Service in the Self-Serve Lane

Look at it this way: when we wish to pump our own gasoline, we pull into the self-service lane. It's economical and we perform many of the tasks that attendants used to do routinely. Well, when we wish to take control of our own lives and to plan our own destinies, we must pull into the self-service lane. We may find that we have been making costly choices by turning some of our life tasks over to others. It might be easier, but there is a price to pay.

Are we not better off making the personal effort, conserving time and resources in the process, to see our goals through to completion? As you read this book, understand its assumption that every time we act positively on our own behalf, we are engaged in self-service. This is true in our professions, relationships, and personal well-being.

The conflict occurs when people remain steeped in a past of self-defeating, and ultimately stifling, lack of creativity. The past keeps us stuck in old patterns and, even worse, entrenched in archaic thinking. When we say—to ourselves or others—"this is the way we've always done it before," we set ourselves up to continue doing the same thing again and again, and of course, we'll get the same results. This philosophy is not only true for those moments of the past that were unsuccessful or unpleasant. Surprisingly, success can also put us into a rut.

James A. Belasco, Ph.D., author of *Teaching the Elephant to Dance,* teaches that even our successes tie us to the past. In fact, he says, "The very factors that produced today's successes create tomorrow's failure." These factors, of course, help keep us from reaching forward to change quickly in order to keep up with the enormous fluctuations going on around us—in our own familiar territory as well as in the entire world. Defeat is the only result. If yesterday's 100-words-per-minute typist hasn't learned computer skills, for example, then we can be fairly certain that he or she is failing in the business world today. The future relies on a present commitment to personal quality and service in all that we do and pursue. Enter the merger of the business and self-help worlds into a complete personal management system.

Quality Mind–Quality Life: A Merging of Worlds

Developing what I call a "quality mind" is the mechanism by which you can merge the best of the self-help and business productivity worlds. It is a way of thinking designed to help you find your special niche in a changing and complex world. It will: 1) help you adopt a quality program in your own life, and 2) assist you in developing the necessary skills for doing so.

The quality mind component involves both *attitudes* and *skills.* The good news is that none of the skills I will discuss in future chapters are unknown to you. To one degree or another, you already possess each of the skills needed to foster a quality mind.

The quality life component involves using attitudes and skills to manage your life effectively. Pursuing a quality life sound simple enough perhaps, but it embodies a powerful set of ideas and concepts that will propel you along the path of personal growth and prosperity. It's a sophisticated partnership of ideas, some born in the personal growth movement, some born in corporate boardrooms.

I think of this move to create quality minds and quality lives as a personal system, one that embraces universal principles but implemented by each of us individually. In that sense, this is a personal management system. "But Paul," my friend Steve said as I described the model to him, "we need something that changes the world, not just ourselves." It is true that some things lie outside the influence of our personal powers. For example, there are others who have greater status and power than we do. Fortunately, we do not need to change other people; we only need to determine what role, if any, they will play in our own lives.

If we base our own personal management programs on the idea that we can change others, we are setting ourselves up for trouble. We start with the premise that we don't have power over other people, we can only change ourselves. But, don't discount the possibility that others will change in the process of our own changes. It's well known that when one person in a relationship changes, the dynamic between them is altered too. I know one thing for certain: Once we appear with the glow that a quality life mind-set brings to us, other people will respond favorably.

Consider Tony. Tony is a man in his late fifties who has worked in several businesses during his career. Tony exhibits the characteristics of a quality life in his demeanor and character. There is the sense of quality given and quality received simply in the way he carries himself. For example, he walks into a restaurant (and I know this because I have been with him) and the staff falls all over him. It becomes quite clear from the way he treats the staff that he maintains a great respect for their role and the important position they hold in relation to his purposes in the restaurant. After all, can he order his dinner without the waiter? Can he get other needs met without the cooperation of the support staff?

Tony knows how to fit the skills of other people within his own goals and purposes. Respect for others exudes from his demeanor, in the expectations he has of the staff, and in the quality his approach delivers to the establishment. He is the epitome of a quality mind–quality life approach because he is aware of his own skills and needs and knows how to evaluate and integrate the skills and roles of others into his own actions.

Consider by contrast, those people who treat flight attendants as personal servants, or who regard store clerks as objects for abuse. There is a skill in recognizing the value in the roles that others serve for your own purpose and intent. This is the first step in translating the model into concrete components of a style that Tony knows how to exercise, an approach which triggers instantaneous response and respect from the other people with whom Tony interacts.

Another outstanding example of a person who exudes quality is my friend and business partner, Chris Salamone, a lawyer who's made a difference. A few years ago, Chris began to think about law school and the life of a law student. Why, he thought, must the three years be so difficult and why do so many people want to become lawyers in the first place? Perhaps, there was a way to screen out those students who would actually be more suited to another career. And, for those who truly have a calling to a legal vocation, was there a way to help them to prosper and succeed in law school?

Chris wanted to bring quality into the law school experience and help those who would be better off doing something else find quality in their lives, too. Underlying all these specifics is Chris's commitment to excellence. In fact, I've never know anyone who embraces the concept of excellence more than Chris. He has famous quotes about excellence posted all over his house—he can't even shave without being reminded of the concept. One could say that excellence is an integral part of Chris's vision.

With his goal to help potential law students, Chris began the National Institute for Legal Education, which holds summer seminars for students *before* they experience their first day of law school. The goal is to turn what could be a miserable three years into a rewarding experience. What was remarkable to me about Chris's effort was the incredibly good use he made of his resources. He enlisted the support from anyone—relative, friends, and colleagues—with something to contribute that would help him launch his project. Knowing that I, too, share a vision of helping people achieve quality in their lives, Chris called on me to work with him at the newly founded institute.

Initially quite successful, this excellent program continued to flourish and expand.

Recently, we've taken the program into high schools with two goals in mind. The first is to help young people decide if a career in the law is for them and second to foster leadership. Chris and I know that our society needs leaders and where better to encourage leaders to emerge than among career-minded high school students. Whether these young people ultimately become lawyers or not, we know we're producing leaders.

My approach to a quality life presupposes that every one of us still has things to learn and always will have more learning to do. The secret is in recognizing how others can help take us to our goals, while operating with a degree of respect for who they are. Absent from our plan is an attitude of abuse, which may move us toward our goal, all the while leaving a trail of enemies.

We weren't born with all the knowledge we need in order to accomplish our goals. In fact, if we already knew exactly what we wanted and precisely how to get there, there would be no need to emphasize quality or management in our personal lives. In order to get what we want from life, we need to expand our skills and abilities, as well as our belief in our potential. This begins by, among other things, treating others with respect for who they are, what they are after, and how they can assist us in reaching our goals.

A quality mind–quality life program is unique in that it starts wherever you are right now and at this moment. I call this your "basepoint." It includes all you have done in the past and it builds on that. We don't have to become different people in order to become motivated to succeed and create the life we want. You do not wipe out your past, you build on it. You are not a failure in search of success. Rather, you build each day from your basepoint, like a business that is changing and expanding to meet the demands of a new marketplace. You are a manager implementing a new plan, relying on your past experiences and present capabilities. From the potential you have at the basepoint, you are prepared to embark on a journey inspired by vision.

The idea of a quality mind incorporates concepts that aren't often found in motivational or "life success" books. For example, why spend time exploring the art of negotiating and decision-making as well as communication, organization, and so on in a book on personal quality? Simply put, because these are the tools upon which our work and personal lives depend. Whatever goal or vision excites you requires that you enhance skills and abilities that are a foundation of almost any life venture—or adventure. These skills are among a world of resources available to you for use as needed. These skills will be discussed later, and taken as a group they are what I call your Resource Inventory (RI).

This book describes a skills-based motivational system beginning at your basepoint and relying on your RI. It won't do much good to walk around seeking quality from yourself and expecting it from others if you are short on the skills that you need to implement your own program. We don't talk our way into the life we want; we must work to create it. Without motivation, our RI remains untapped and will eventually wither and decay. Without a developed skills inventory, our drive or motivation doesn't get us very far.

If we were all actively engaged in practicing "quality thinking," there would be an attitude of respect from others as we make clear what we expect of them. Our self-respect would be evident in our confidence and clear direction. Others would know what we were capable of giving back to them. Of course, quality thinking means you will no longer blame others for your own shortcomings and failures. Implement this way of viewing your life and watch whatever weaknesses you have float away, replaced by quality.

Taking the First Step

Think for a minute about the people you most admire. Do they blame other people, because now, at age 35 or 45 or 55 they haven't accomplished their goals or dreams? Or, do they take responsibility for their own lives? Looking at the corporate world from which much of this material comes, consider whether we get farther by emulating the business leaders who whine about the Japanese, or working with those who recognize the need to do better here and win back our competitive edge through hard work? You probably prefer to be around people who take personal responsibility for their lives. So, don't be afraid to evaluate how you manage yourself. Do others get your best efforts? Do you demand or expect the best from others? Do you have a sense of vision, but lack a plan for how to get there—so you end up not getting anywhere? The answer lies in understanding the role that others play in your life. (You can view these people as suppliers of the resources you may need from time to time to resolve problems or to assist in personal growth).

Take these people and the gifts they can offer you into every interaction; exude the confidence that accompanies the knowledge that you know how to combine all of the people and other resources available to you as you work to grow personally. You should get a sense of the keen awareness you need of your own abilities and those of others upon whom you can rely.

The more difficult challenge of this book is the need for you to constantly evaluate your beliefs, actions, goals, and past results. For example, you may absorb the notion that the harder you work the more successful you will be. Unfortunately, the frustration you feel when your hard work just keeps you running in place confirms the need to explore and reject the status quo and the assumption that hard work guarantees rewards.

In the next chapter, you'll learn the historical framework within which the quality life model emerges. It concludes by discussing the importance of creating a vision from which each path of life's journey can be followed. Chapter Three sets out the specific components of this new integrated system for change. Once the system is laid out, I will assist you in applying the model to the key phases and processes of your life, and then we'll look at the skills you can develop as you develop your quality mind program.

The world has changed; the same beliefs you have held in the past will not likely be sufficient to get you where you wish to go. This book will help you see your life as a process. It will help you set goals and develop and use important skills necessary to reach them. And it will also help you integrate all aspects of your life.

You aren't really a different person at home and at work. You are the same person using different elements of the same skills to make your way in both worlds. Shifting your attitudes and taking responsibility for living your life creatively isn't simply a nice thing to do. More likely than not, it is part of an essential belief system to live successfully in the future.

This book is for the reader who wishes to be part of making positive and directive changes towards a balance both professionally and personally—I invite you to read on.

CHAPTER II

Quality Life Management

IF YOU'RE LIKE MOST PEOPLE, you're frustrated with situations that surround you—poor service, defective products, fear of being punished for making mistakes, fear of failure, being blamed for what isn't your fault, and so on. You decry waste and lack of quality at the highest levels of government, corporations, and financial institutions. Perhaps you are out of work yourself, trying to gather the courage to start rebuilding your life again. Or, maybe your life appears to be stagnant—you're going nowhere, or worse yet, backwards.

The range of our concerns is vast, and its impact on our lives profound. At times, we feel isolated or ill-prepared to confront the challenges that face us personally and professionally. There is nothing abnormal about this; the issue is whether you let life control you, or whether you seek to exert some control over life.

Not long ago I quit my job as Assistant Dean of a law school in Chicago. I left the security of that position (not to mention its steady paycheck) in order to pursue my own road to happiness, lecturing and presenting programs across the country and using my legal expertise by appearing as media legal consultant or correspondent. Perhaps my change doesn't seem very powerful to you (other people's changes often don't), but consider what it took. From my perspective, we're talking guts! I earned decent money, had respect, recognition, and all those things which a professional position supplies. Yet, I felt out of control of my life—I needed and wanted empowerment to achieve my own destiny. Giving up all of that security for a shot at a different kind of success, and with the hope that someone out there would be willing to read this book, or listen to a lecture—and *pay me* in the process—was indeed a risk. Add to this risk the mortgage, utilities, car payments, and a host of other bills, and the dangers appeared even greater.

Then I remembered a conversation I had with my mother when I was quite young. "What do you really want to do when you're older?" she asked me.

"I want to be a public speaker and write books, Mom," I answered with a gleam in my eye.

"Great, so you'll go give a speech and you'll write books..." she responded with a hint of a laugh in her tone. You see, she couldn't quite form a clear picture of who would show up for the talk, why people would want to read my books, or what topics I would be addressing. Ah, but a mother's love is indeed supportive. I'm not sure I had any better answers at the time either, but I knew the dream was in place. I just needed to figure out how to get there.

Did I make it? Well, I'm not sure I am there completely, but I have pursued my goals and made a commitment to quality in my life. In addition to using my legal expertise in a number of consulting situations, I also became NBC's legal consultant on jury selection for the O.J. Simpson trial, which gave me numerous opportunities for on-camera work. So, was that a lucky break? Sure, conventional wisdom would say I was lucky. But would that have happened if I'd stayed at my job in Chicago? No, that opportunity came when I'd made the leap or taken the plunge—pick your own expression. I was at the right place at the right time because I was moving in the direction of my goals.

I haven't completely "arrived" because I am constantly reviewing, analyzing, and considering new ways I can increase the quality in my own life. When I've reached one goal, I think of ways to improve on it. Certainly, I permit moments of satisfaction and fulfillment in my life, but I never lose sight of the fact that there is always the potential for more growth and greater prosperity.

My experience is probably much like that of others who have made up their minds to make a big change. The seed might have been planted early in life, and then at some point, they believed they were ready to make the move. I knew that a component of my goals involves helping others make the moves necessary for them to move ahead.

Upon learning that I decided to go to work for myself, my friend Julie gave me a powerful message that I came to learn was more true than I might ever have guessed. "Good luck, buddy," she said. "You're now working for the world's worst S.O.B." I knew that the comment wasn't a reflection of how I had previously treated my staff at the law school—at least I hoped not. Rather, the comment was meant to drive home a different reality: No one can expect more from you than you. No one understands your potential, your skills, or your resources better than you. We are inevitably our own toughest, but, in a world emphasizing quality, the best boss possible. And the boss always knows when resources are mismanaged, ignored, or otherwise frittered away. In simple terms, it's known as waste.

Waste Not, Want Not

Waste is all around us. But, it can serve as a link between current frustrations and the shift we seek toward quality in our personal lives. Philip Crosby, a quality expert, business consultant, and book author emphasizes in his work that poor quality is ultimately expensive. He believes, and has shown again and again, that prevention is far more economical than funding a cure. It takes far more time to act, detect error, create a "fix" for the problem, and implement it, than to plan properly in the first place and execute the plan the correct way the first time.

As I read Crosby, I realized that the principles so well proven to create quality in business should be the source of personal quality empowerment as well.

According to Crosby, morale tends to be high when quality is sought the first time around. Japanese management takes a similar attitude in its recognition that wasted time and materials result in negative consequences for the whole society. This is a subtle, but important premise. Basically, a sloppy attitude toward quality translates to a sloppy attitude toward people and disrespect for their worth. We could also argue that this disrespect results in a sloppy attitude toward the earth and its resources, too.

American managers are now changing their attitudes. It's now generally recognized that using time to correct mistakes or doing the same jobs twice or more is time lost. This waste seems so common in our personal lives that it is difficult to imagine how it could have been missed by previous theorists in the self-help movement. Let us overlook this issue no more.

How many times have you cursed yourself for an avoidable mistake, knowing that the job just had to be done over? Think of how you feel when you are a customer having to return a defective item to the store and the sense that the frustration and wasted time could have been avoided had quality been a part of the sales process. And, right you are to feel that way—so refuse to stand for it anymore! Seek quality—but first, define it for yourself.

What is this Thing Called "Quality?"

Quality is what most of us say we want in the people and products in our lives. We all seem to know what others mean when they talk about this concept called quality. Quality is often hard to define, but we know it when we see it. For some, it's money—for others it's power or recognition. In any case—in *every* case—it's peace of mind and satisfaction with our situation in life. In fact, most of us would agree that we want to live a quality life.

Although we can't often articulate it, we know when we're living a quality life, and when we're not, it's time for *us* to do something different. When we feel our energy and enthusiasm draining away from us, it usually means that we are not living a quality life. The converse is true as well. When we are living a high quality life, we have energy to spare and people like to be around us because of our enthusiasm. Am I making sense? Can you sense the truth of what I'm saying?

I borrow the concept of quality from the business community and apply it to our personal lives because I realize that these worlds aren't so separate after all. Today's business community has a sense of urgency about change and the need for a shift to quality production and delivery of goods and services. One of the primary precepts of instituting a quality program in businesses is that it must be done *now;* there is no time for lengthy studies and endless meetings.

As individuals, shouldn't we have the same sense of urgency about our own lives? What are we waiting for? Can you come up with one good reason that justifies not gaining control over the quality of your own life? If you can, you're not yet in touch with your already powerful existing resources, or you think the challenge is all talk with no clarity.

Perhaps much of the literature you've read about personal change has seemed a bit esoteric, full of theories that are difficult to apply. But this book is different. The quality mind–quality life concept is meant to be the *concrete* mechanism needed to start a program of change. By relying on the substantive steps used by the business community, we can now say that the days of well-intentioned, but hard to apply material are over. Finally, a model is offered to you that carries the spirit necessary to motivate you, but also provides clear direction.

Roots: Where did Quality Come From?

The quality movement in the United States was born in manufacturing, rapidly spread to other types of businesses, and now belongs in the world of personal growth. Always targeted to the management community, growth seems to be the responsibility of the people who are in charge of quality programs and policies.

Managers implement a plan, check on its progress, identify snags, iron out the difficulties, analyze the results, and write the reports. They choose suppliers and vendors and see to it that the product is packaged and reaches the end user—whether other businesses, or you and me. Managers make demands on others, ask for help and advice, and give credit to others where it's due. (Doesn't this sound like a description of a job you hold whether you asked for it or not, whether you do it poorly or well, or even if you have abdicated the role?)

A bit of personal reflection led me to realize that I already am, and need to be, the manager in my own life. It's up to me whether I do this job poorly or well. Have you ever taken a moment to consider who is the manager in your life? Do conditions and other people rule and manage your decisions and direction? Do you have the will to take over that task by introducing quality into the process?

You see, "manager" is more than a title. The verb "to manage" means exerting control and establishing direction. The end product of managing, or management, is the specific responsibility to be fulfilled using a combination of logic and creativity. To manage means to get results efficiently and, we assume, using the skills and techniques learned first theoretically, and then through practice. The foundation of good business practice should be the cornerstone of personal growth.

Once we accept the responsibility to manage our own lives, we can begin to learn and use a new language of life management. For example, think how often we hear people say self-defeating things like, "Well, I've lived through the week," or, "I forced myself to stay awake in class, but I don't think the professor noticed what a struggle it was."

Imagine how much different our lives would be if we talked about how we managed ourselves during the week. What if we said, "Well, I managed myself pretty well this week," or, "I managed my day so well that I was able to be alert for my night class. In fact, the professor responded clearly to all my questions." *Personal* management is one important dimension here, and ultimately, our satisfaction in life depends on our ability to manage ourselves in a high-quality manner.

Consider what life could be like if we began to expect quality management from others? What if we, like corporate managers, began to use only those resources that promised and delivered quality? One woman I know walked out of her (now former) physician's office because she was treated rudely on the telephone when she called for an appointment. Then she was kept waiting more than an hour—for the third time in a row—without an apology from the staff. "Well, that's typical" is only an acceptable reflection on these circumstances if you're willing to settle for the status quo. I urge you to reach higher.

A quality-oriented mind means immediately returning merchandise that fails to meet our quality expectations, and talking to managers in stores when service is poor, and registering complaints in restaurants when food is badly prepared. Ultimately, it means letting others know when they are not adding quality to our lives and deciding whether they can remain part of our quest for a quality life. There might be some hard choices in front of us, but most of the time we only lose what we really didn't want in the first place.

One of the reasons the quality movement has spread from manufacturing to retail and service businesses is that for many Americans, good service has become more than a dream. The business manager's message is clear: We either deliver a quality service (or product) or we fail. As managers of our own lives, we should expect the same commitment from ourselves and from others who are part of our lives. A good "product" should be presumed; excellence in service and in every other respect is also an entitlement.

When I talk about changing our lives, I envision a world in which we give and receive quality; one in which we all assume responsibility for managing ourselves. If these words are heeded, the result is a world of empowered people, propelled through personal quality management. It is a world of people empowering themselves and each other.

We can also think about personal management to bring about a quality life as a system. Why not just a program, or a plan, or even a technique? Because the concept of a system better reflects the results when individual parts become integrated into a unified whole. Frankly, we have all had enough of other people's quick success programs and plans that often fall flat in days or weeks. Those systems impose requirements and restrictions often unnatural to us. A quality system relies on and builds upon resources already available to you. This system provides for flexibility and the capacity for fine tuning it to your individual needs and goals. Just as two businesses can employ different quality management systems, a quality life system for two individuals will be unique to each.

If you live with another person who is also interested in quality mind—quality life ideas, then each of you will adapt this system to suit your own individual needs. Your partner will come up with a similar plan. Consider yourself lucky if people around you also use this system. You will live and work in greater harmony when you are speaking the same "quality life" language. Your personal success lies in the specific steps necessarily taken to create a fluid quality system.

Each part of a quality mind–quality life system serves a purpose, but carries far less meaning until it is viewed as one of many integrated features. So, you can't short-circuit the road to quality in life. The old adage may express it best: The whole is greater than the sum of its parts. As you read on, understand that what is being sought is a broad, all encompassing, smoothly functioning system. Your results will be all encompassing as well.

Since this approach relies significantly on the substance of the quality movement in business and industry, it would serve to complete the foundation and framework of my system with a brief history of the quality movement. The application is an easy next step.

An Accident of History

The modern quality movement grew, quite literally, out of the tragedy and rubble of World War II, and blossomed in answer to the changing world of the late post-war era. In both Japan and Europe, massive destruction required an equally massive rebuilding job. The rest is history. Quality became an enormous issue in the U.S. corporate environment as we watched Japan, with the help of some key Americans, become the role model for industrial success and economic stability. A commitment to quality underlies this success.

The first step in considering how a quality system works involves examining the success the Japanese have experienced in recent decades. Of course, we must recognize that the quality movement exists apart from political issues or cultures. Still, the work of the Japanese needs to be considered as an integral part of the quality philosophy. Interestingly enough, much of what constitutes quality in Japanese production has been extended into the individual Japanese person's way of life.

When you hear people discussing U.S.-Japanese relations, these issues often become entangled with hostility and competitiveness. The quality movement is *not* about what is wrong with American standards or right with the Japanese production method. On the contrary, the quality issue has to do with what the Japanese business community has been doing *better* than their American counterparts.

One of the interesting accidents of history is that it was Americans who were initially responsible for helping the Japanese develop their commitment to increased productivity and their emphasis on quality. Although many brilliant individuals were involved, two names have emerged as acknowledged founders—some call them legends—of the modern quality movement. W. Edwards Deming and J.M. Juran both played unique roles in Japan's industrial success. Their work now serves as the foundation for many of the quality programs in the U.S. and is also the foundation for a quality mind–quality life attitude.

W. Edwards Deming is the creator of statistical quality control (SQC), a system that leads to the concept of zero defects. Deming's work with Japanese industries in the early 1950s resulted in creating a national prize and naming it after him. The Deming Prize is a coveted award given by the Japanese to companies who have shown not only a commitment to quality, but have used a quality program to get results. Deming lived into his 90s, and his influence has spread to every corner of the globe. It is difficult to talk about quality without thinking of Deming.

Perhaps the most important concept that Deming brought to the quality movement was the notion that we have a right to find joy in our work. His commitment to quality eliminated a belief in the necessity for a grim and grinding workforce. Keep this concept of joy in the forefront of your mind as you develop a quality program that reflects your right to find and even exploit joy in your work and daily life.

A distinguished reputation also accompanies the name of J.M. Juran, known as the creator of total quality control (TQC). While Deming's system appeared to be more applicable to industrial production, Juran's system involves everyone in an organization. A quality life attitude involves everyone in our personal network—at work, at play, and in family.

To illustrate what the quality movement means today, and how it differs from the so-called quality control operations of the past, consider this: Motorola announced a previously unheard of goal—60 defects or less for every billion components it produces. This is essentially a goal of zero defects, which simply put, means that there is no variation in production. There is one way to do it, one goal, and there is no *range* of acceptability. The product either meets the specifications or it does not.

Perhaps this standard sounds reasonable to you, but in business production, it sent shockwaves through the management community. This approach was not the norm for American business. In the past, American business viewed quality as something that was checked and controlled *after* the fact. For example, a relatively loose system was set up to insure an acceptable level of quality in each step of production. Then, when the product was finished, quality was checked and those parts or products that were defective were sent back to be fixed.

This doesn't sound too different from the way in which many people live their lives, does it? Consider that we often act before we think, and deal with the consequences later. We often settle for what is "good enough," not demanding higher quality from our own work. We even understand when others cannot meet our expectations, accepting excuses and shortcomings. Would it seem reasonable to demand more? To expect more? Well, to date, it just isn't done that way.

Yesterday Won't Do Today

Let's not judge our standards without putting them into perspective. Look first to U.S. business practices in order to put the traditional quality control system into an historical perspective. After World War II, the U.S. was the industrial capital of the world. We didn't have much competition; the demand for our products was so great that quantity became more important than quality.

It was rather simple: the toaster that didn't work when you got it home, the car that turned out to be a lemon, the building materials that weren't cut correctly, and on and on, were simply considered part of the "normal" results of production. If it didn't turn out right, then we spent time to fix it, or returned it and got another—which may or may not have worked.

There were those who pushed for quality, but it still revolved around improving a process here or there or tinkering with the production line. Until the 1980s, the notion of zero defects, quality programs that involved everyone, and the concept of exceptional service simply didn't get talked about in boardrooms. In fact, the push for quantity production, with quality de-emphasized, actually served the United States well for decades—or so it seemed.

Unfortunately, the push for quantity only, accompanied by the high profits it produced, spoiled Americans in some ways. We tended to forget that other people in the world have skills, creativity, motivation, and all the rest of the assets that built our country into an innovative giant.

Although we aren't responsible for the old trends and the mistakes of the past, we now live with the results. Furthermore, we are responsible for our part in the future of the country and of ourselves. The same proverbial "American ingenuity and know-how" that we are so famous for has served us well in the past; it will do so again.

A quality-mind attitude demands that we no longer be content with "satisfactory." Rather than living with error, begin to ask yourself whether you look at mistakes as something you can and do go back in and fix after the fact, or if you might find better ways to avoid them in the first place. Certainly, human beings aren't machines. We can't live our lives demanding zero defects, or walking a narrow path of believing that there is only one acceptable way to do things. On the contrary, prosperity results from the choices available to us at any one time. Growth lies in the variety of opportunities available to us—whether we are conscious of them or not.

Our quality mind begins with a first step. For many of us, it might be as simple as knowing that we waste precious time looking for things because we haven't put them away. For others, it might be a more complex examination of the way we allow others to block our dreams or make unreasonable demands that we end up resenting. In essence, are we allowing other people to add "defects" to our own process of life production, contaminating it—and us—in an important way?

The enormous growth of the quality movement in American business is wonderful news because it holds the promise of launching America on a new course, a new adventure that will shape the future. Now that same quality movement can be brought into your personal life, launching you on a new course and new adventure that can shape your own future.

Why take the step? America once ignored the rapid growth of economies in the rest of the world. We soon (it seemed almost overnight) had competition and were at a loss for a response. Even worse, our products, once the source of great pride, were now being criticized. Customers didn't want to send one out of four parts back so that defects could be corrected; customers didn't like waiting for delivery.

Other non-American companies began to send *quality* parts on time. American business could sleep no more.

Consider similar questions in your own life. Are other people getting the jobs for which you applied? Did someone else get your account because a competitor beat you to the punch? Did you lose a spouse or lover because your partner believed that you were no longer present in the relationship and the caring atmosphere was gone? Not unlike the problems that lead American production forces to seek quality in their production efforts, individuals are coming to see the need to seek personal quality in their own life to regain control over interactions and relationships.

Quality begins with service to the self. Throughout the post-World War II decades, we were told that the shift to a service economy would make defects in manufacturing irrelevant. Of course, those of us who have suffered the profound lack of service in our so-called service economy find it difficult to agree. Unfortunately, the attitude that quality can be fixed later seeped into the service and information industries. Does this describe the way you live your life currently? Stay tuned, because you *can* change all that.

Change sometimes seems slow and laborious. The quality movement demands that time *not* be on our side. We either get on the bandwagon or we watch it pass us by. Those who have become part of this movement—perhaps without even calling it that—have become well known.

Consider, for example, Frederick Smith, the founder and chief executive of Federal Express. He has become a legend for founding a company known for excellent service. Interestingly enough, his description of a "100 percent customer satisfaction overnight delivery service" received a "C" on a paper he wrote in school. His teacher found the proposal to be impossible. While Smith did not institute a quality program as such in his company, he devised a training program that, in essence, turned the day-to-day decisions of the business over to its employees. His program puts the responsibility for the company's performance into the hands of the people who actually carry out the work.

Smith replaced, "I have to speak to my supervisor," with instructions to employees to come up with a solution themselves—without red tape and without delay. Quality includes learning the mechanics of creating solutions and a personal management attitude that makes each of us his or her own boss. For Federal Express, every day represents an opportunity to satisfy every customer; the goal is 100 percent customer satisfaction. Individual employees may do whatever it takes to make that happen—absolutely and positively!

When I first began to think of the applications of the quality movement to our personal lives, Smith's attitude about his employees seemed an integral part of the formula. A quality-oriented life requires trust, an incredible amount of trust, in ourselves and in those with whom we interact and who play a role in our lives. Trust starts with training and education until we come to understand our goals and the personal mechanics of crafting the road to reaching it.

When you think about it, it seems amazing that Federal Express employees have enough faith in management that they aren't afraid of being fired when they make decisions on their own. Smith's goal becomes their goal too; punishment should not result from taking responsibility. Can you say this about your life at work? At home? Are you letting fear of failure block you from creating and pursuing your road to personal happiness?

Another unfortunate reality is our fear of economic insecurity. For many people, there is nothing more frightening than losing a job. We often believe that with one wrong move, we'll be fired. Rather than fostering creativity and taking responsibility, many people run scared, so to speak, and do nothing out of the ordinary. They stick to the rule book, and advise others to do the same. But that system encourages the status quo.

Creativity and trust must play a role in success because the late 1980s, a time when the climate of fear was widespread, saw the number of new *small* businesses grow dramatically. In fact, I would imagine that many of you have started, or long to start, a business of your own. The longing for independence has been rekindled in this country, because the notion of life-long security with a company is no longer a reality anyway.

A business of my own was one of my dreams as well, and fulfilling that dream has been one of the most gratifying experiences of my life. My goal of working on-camera was reached when I opened myself up to that possibility. And the convergence of my hard work and circumstances enabled me to reach that dream, too. While I can't claim that my educational environment had the negative climate found in many corporations, I experienced it when I practiced law. Most important, like Fred Smith's employees, I wanted to feel in charge of my work. In fact, I *demanded* control and quality in every phase of my life. Those of you who have that same drive to exert as much control as possible over your destiny will no doubt relate to my desire. Without it, we coast along at idle speed, trapped in whatever life phase won't let us out—until we exercise the quality demand.

Corporations often decry the lack of loyalty among their employees, while simultaneously creating in those employees a sense of being expendable, a sense that has permeated almost every factory, service industry, school, and government agency. Fortunately, there are many people in the business world who know that an entire shift in attitude is needed; quality programs will lead the way to a fresh, new climate in employee-employer relations and in your personal relations as well.

For most of us, it takes little to become discouraged about making changes in life. We are often quick to accept that we are too old, too young, not well educated, not talented enough, too burdened with responsibility, and on and on. Some people smother their potential by describing themselves as not "good enough." What a wasteful attitude. So, it's time to get a new attitude— time to begin your change towards a life of total quality; do so first by establishing a vision to guide you toward success.

Getting Started: Beyond Goals to Creating Vision

In *Teaching the Elephant to Dance,* James Belasco explains the way in which vision drives action. An organization or an individual with a vision attracts support from others. A vision can create a sense of urgency, a sense that the plan needs to start *today.* It is a guiding principle, encompassing our goals. A vision has implications that reach farther than a goal, which has an end point as well as a starting place. Belasco quotes Father Theodore Hesburgh, the president of Notre Dame University for 35 years and the man responsible for making it an important academic institution. "The very essence of leadership is you have to have a vision. It's got to be a vision you articulate clearly and forcefully on every occasion. You can't blow an uncertain trumpet."

Belasco goes on to say that a vision "... identifies clearly for all concerned—employees, customers, and suppliers—exactly what an organization stands for and precisely why they should support it." If a company has a vision, if cities and countries have visions, then shouldn't individuals have them too? If success is your desire, then a vision is a prerequisite.

It might seem like a simple concept, but can you define your vision as you sit and read this book? Do you really know what you stand for? Do the people around you—coworkers, family, friends— know what you stand for and why and how they should support you? In personal terms, do people say, "I know what you're about?" Think of people in your life who appear to have a vision. They may not call it that, but they are just quietly—or not so quietly—going about the business of living with a purpose, with or without a sense of total quality. The goal here is to create a vision and then pursue it with quality surrounding and propelling your every effort.

I recently heard about a woman named Karen, who supports her family with a job as a school teacher—and she is a very dedicated and talented one. However, three nights each week and every Saturday, Karen goes to her studio to produce her own art. She does this because she has a vision and unless she works to fulfill it, she feels dead inside. Karen's vision is simple: "I am an artist who expresses life's meaning through my work, and I give back my vision to people who appreciate and enjoy what I create."

Karen doesn't waste her energy complaining about not having enough time or about the lack of support from some family members—and she has contended with some painful griping from her family, who wants her home more of the time. She goes about her life with the determination of one who knows who she is and where she stands. She is guided by her vision. Because Karen is clear about her vision, her family has learned to understand what she is after—what is important to the quality in her life—and they have learned to adjust.

My good friend Jim devotes most of his time volunteering at a clinic that treats people with AIDS. Jim leads group discussions for people with AIDS, and serves as a support person for individual patients. He is there when they want to talk, or need support, or just feel the need to know that someone cares about them.

Jim won't do this all his life. The work is emotionally draining and difficult, and he watches as these clients, who often become friends, weaken in body and spirit until they die. As noble as his efforts are, he also has other goals and plans for himself. However, rather than doing only part-time volunteer work, he decided to commit to three years of volunteer effort while he supports himself by working as a church choir director and organist. Friends have urged him not to sacrifice such time, saying that he risks not meeting his own career goals; others openly disapprove of his current path.

To Jim's credit, however, everyone knows where he stands. He has a vision that he can easily explain to those who care to be a part of his quality life. Simply put, he wants to be of service to those who need help right now. His specific work is the vehicle to carry out that service. Jim is guided by his vision.

It's important to remember that a vision is not the same thing as a goal or a plan. Remember my friend who had never created a vision because she was afraid she wouldn't like it once she got it? Well, she had visions and goals confused. To create a quality life, first think about your mission or purpose. Successful companies do this; successful individuals can do this too.

According to Belasco, IBM's vision is to provide the best customer service. They may make a quality business machine, but isn't that just the vehicle? If IBM changed its products, it would still have the same vision. Are you beginning to see how this works?

Almost all institutions have visions; those that don't are unlikely to do their chosen tasks very well. Politicians like to move us with their vision. In fact, it's been said that even though we give lip service to learning about issues, we really vote for a person, not a policy. That's why candidates use the word vision so much. They want us to imagine along with them. It's as if we have more trust in a person who says, "I may not have all the answers, but I know where I'd like to go."

The sticky part comes in when they—and we—realize that they don't have the faintest idea how to get us anywhere near that vision. We could say that many politicians have given vision a bad name. But we can change that too, if we all have a vision in our own lives.

My friend Judy equates vision with a life purpose. Rather than describing her vision in specific terms—that would too easily sound the same as goals—she thinks about why she is on this planet. What does she want to do except take up space? What is her life about? When she looks back on it, how have her skills, resources, relationships, and actions made a difference? In Judy's case, her life purpose has been summed up in a simple phrase: "I support other people, using my own skills and abilities, as they search within themselves."

Judy happens to be a career counselor. She helps people search for satisfying careers and helps them develop skills to use when looking for new positions. But, Judy could be a minister or a therapist, just to give two examples. She carries out her life purpose in a particular, practical, tangible way, but the structure is a framework from which she lives her purpose.

I know other people who describe their purposes—or visions—as entertaining others, instructing others, expressing, nurturing, and so on. An actor friend who wants to entertain could be a dancer or a poet. However, his particular medium is theater. The person whose purpose is expression happens to be a writer, but she could just as well have been a painter.

Vision is a loose concept, not necessarily tied to a specific framework. When we view it as a quality, a concept, or a mission, we can see the endless possibilities.

Earlier, I mentioned W. Edward Deming's vision of a company in which all employees found joy in their work. Contrary to much of the philosophical foundation of capitalism, Deming believed joy in work to be a basic right. He also believed that competition among workers and traditional hierarchies destroyed this potential for joy. If we apply Deming's ideas to the personal realm, the message becomes clear.

We need not compete with anyone else, nor must we tailor our vision to those of other people. We are each unique; we all possess the right to our own vision and the pursuit of personal happiness, whatever that means for us.

Implementing a quality program takes time, and isn't always easy. But according to many of this country's finest business minds, it is absolutely necessary if we are going to compete in the international marketplace of the future, both professionally and personally.

It's that simple, it's that terrifying, but it's that promising. Devising a quality program does not mean merely tinkering with our existing philosophies. On the contrary, establishing a system of quality in our personal lives requires examining and adopting an entirely new philosophy. It requires commitment, vision, and high individual performance standards.

In the workplace or at home, a quality program can't be a sometime thing, a policy that is turned on and off, or in which only a portion of the employees or family members participate. It involves a whole-hearted commitment to implement changes—not overnight, because that would overwhelm the most energetic among us—but one action, one plan, one day at a time. This is the guarantee for success and it is precisely why I believe it is essential in a personal pursuit of happiness.

Creating Your Own Vision

Before we move on, it is important that you establish a vision for your own life. Take some time and write out a vision for yourself and your life. It need not be elaborate or permanent or even well-defined right now. However, it will serve as part of your own basepoint, the place from which you begin the challenge of exploring the quality mind concept. It will serve as a touchstone, a reminder of the reasons you have for making the effort to strive for quality in your life.

Perhaps your vision is to help others grow, or to have satisfactory relationships, or to see "the forest through the trees of life." A simple phrase, a clear directive is all that is needed. This theme will become your guide, through each individual decision you make, each life step you take. Along the path you will have your vision, and everything else will clear that path you choose to walk.

It's important that your vision give you a light, energetic feeling in your whole being. Never should a vision become burdensome or limiting. On the contrary, your vision serves as the guiding light that keeps you on course as you tap into all you already know and all the resources you already have available to you in your resource inventory (RI). You will use your vision to build on the potential that exists deep inside you as you reach for what you want in your life. There will be many options for how you will realize and live your vision—as the person who seeks to help others can just as easily become a counselor as a flight attendant or writer.

Right now you are on the path to controlling your own destiny from the best possible starting point—exactly where you are at this moment. So take this moment and write your vision down. Post it on the bathroom mirror, the refrigerator, the garage door, and wherever else it is likely to remind you of the challenge you have accepted to achieve prosperity.

Surely the prospect of establishing quality in your life—in all areas of your life—can seem overwhelming. Rest assured that there is little need to be intimidated by the challenge. You already possess the skills to develop a quality mind and live a quality life. Just as U.S. industry has the resources to implement a quality program, so you have the resources for personal development.

You will not begin from ground zero; you begin right where you are—here and now. And, you will soon see that you already have many internal and external tools and resources at your disposal. The next chapter works from the vision you establish in order to set out the specific components of your personal quality plan.

VISION—We've talked about how important it is. Having a vision precedes goals and plans. It's a simple statement of what you are about, the underlying purpose of your life. Take a few minutes and think about your vision. Then write it down here. You can refer to it often to remind you that you're going to evaluate your choices and actions based on their compatibility with your vision.

MY VISION IS:

_____

_____

_____

_____

_____

_____

_____

_____

_____

CHAPTER III

There's No Place Like Home:
Fundamentals of Quality Thinking

I'VE ALWAYS BEEN FASCINATED by the hope and enthusiasm that motivational speakers appear to evoke in the audience who attend their speeches. Even more, I have wondered why the new spirited enthusiasm and motivation seem to last but a few days, after which the motivation fades into the background. The problems and issues that sent those people to the seminar in the first place begin to take over again.

Several years ago I attended a motivational seminar held in a large hotel just outside of Chicago. Arriving a bit early, as I often do, I did a bit of "people watching," and with nearly 300 or so people gathering in the large ballroom, there were lots of people to watch.

The crowd was a mixture of men and women who were white, black, Hispanic, and Asian American—and they came in all shapes and sizes. In fact, as a group, they represented a fair sampling of what our country looks like. An outsider looking in might have assumed that this group of people were seeking a cure, but weren't quite sure what ailed them. Somewhere there was the right answer, and that night they were there to find it.

The air was filled with anticipation as we waited for the well-known speaker to arrive. As is my habit at events like this, I wandered through the crowd and did a bit of, if the truth be told, eavesdropping. Some people had come in groups. There were many couples, or groups of two or three friends, and even what appeared to be three

generations of the same family. It was a friendly, talkative group, typical of motivational program audiences. In fact, I saw many people
wander in by themselves and as they claimed a seat, they became
drawn into conversations already in progress. There was no room for
loneliness or isolation in this gregarious crowd.

Some of the things I heard while I meandered around the room
were nothing short of surprising, given that these people had no previous history with each other. It's amazing how people become open
with total strangers when they are in an atmosphere of hope. They discussed the reasons they had decided to attend this event and they
talked in general terms about life. I guess this parallels our willingness
to bare our souls to others on trains and airplanes. That same trust gets
triggered in the fast intimacy of a motivational seminar.

The prevailing theme within that crowd can be summed up as
"expand, grow, do, and be all you can be." On the surface, this optimistic and motivational theme ran through the comments I heard as
I listened to and chatted with the seminar attenders. But then, I asked
myself, "Was this what was really being said? Was I missing something
important?"

"My life isn't working," I heard a man in a neat business suit and
wire-rimmed glasses say. I imagine he was an executive who was trying to balance work with the rest of his life. "This speaker is supposed
to be good. I hope he can help me get started," was another comment,
this one made by a woman with a professional appearance, who was
also quite outspoken and warm. I was wondering what it was she
needed to get started on when she added, "and I'm just about broke."
Ah... a new business venture most likely.

Another person in the group shook his head in agreement, and
said, "I know how that is. I'm just about broke too, and I can't seem
to figure out what's wrong with me." I wondered why financial difficulty seemed to equate with total personal failure. What natural tie

is there between life's difficulties and assassinating one's own character? From the tone of these comments, I might have thought that this was a group of homeless people, or at least a convention of the long-term unemployed.

But it was clear that despite their social tone of voice, these people were confused, discouraged, and in some cases, actually depressed. Here they were, mostly well-dressed, well-fed—even to the point of looking like the so-called "beautiful people"—but they had, in many cases, made a long trip to hear a speaker who would presumably motivate them to get their lives back in order.

Didn't the power exist within them already? It had to, or the night would be wasted. There was nothing any speaker, no matter how charismatic, could say that could create the type of personal and specific change these listeners needed and wanted.

I've thought a lot about the way so many of the people I saw that night talked about themselves and their lives. To be sure, many of these people were aware that their lives were not total disasters. In fact, underlying each of their concerns was the positive desire to improve and grow. And why not? I give these quite likeable strangers a lot of credit for being able to admit to their feelings of dissatisfaction.

Many people—too many people—had come to this seminar believing, at least on some level, that they hadn't yet accomplished *anything* in their lives, or what they had done wasn't done successfully. Yet, I came to learn that the vast majority of the people in that room were holding down responsible jobs, more than 50 percent had been to college, many were there with spouses or partners, and a substantial number had raised children or were still in that process. So why was there such a prevailing need for outside help?

Perhaps the problems these people perceived had to do with vision. Is it possible that they spent time thinking about goals and plans, but without a guiding principle that served as a foundation for the whole of life? Could they be living without vision?

A Quality Mind Journey

Keep that room full of people in mind as you read on. If you're one of those people who looks ahead at the chapter titles (and if you aren't, loosen up, and do it) you know that throughout the book I will be talking about change that can happen now, with a focus on resources and skills available to you today. The very personal answer lies in your recognition and demand for quality in your life. Quality is what you should be all about. Quality is what this book is all about. Skills such as communication, decision-making, negotiation, and conflict resolution will come into play in your personal quality system— skills you already have inside you.

You will not pursue this journey from scratch. You already have experiences and information from which to start. Perhaps you are not currently where you want to be, but chances are, you worked hard to get to wherever you are today, frustrations and all. With all of the good times and the difficult moments and challenges you have faced, it is valuable to take a moment, close your eyes, and thank yourself for all that you have accomplished. This is the beginning point of growth and prosperity.

Now fit your world of experience, your *basepoint,* into a framework which will guide your journey to personal quality. It is important that you accept the precepts of the system, and so they are set out as "rules," which simply means they have force behind them. Failure to recognize or follow them means difficulty in pursuing the road to quality. Respect for the foundation that they create means a more swift journey towards personal quality.

Rule One: Speak Positively about Your Past and Present with an Eye Toward the Future.

… And this means without punishment for what has *not yet* happened, and without concern for an unknown future. Rather, take a moment of pleasure to thank yourself for the years of thought, analysis, schooling, work, and street experience. And thank anything and anyone else who has helped you arrive at wherever you are today. Reflect—appreciate—and see the glory of today. We grow from our conflicts and our difficulties.

The problem I saw among so many people at that seminar was their lack of appreciation for what they had already created in their lives. Perhaps they were afraid to give themselves credit; perhaps doing so would appear arrogant or boastful. But true self-appreciation is neither. Self-appreciation implies living consciously and with a *purpose.*

It should be easy to see why I have named your current life status as your *"basepoint."* It includes everything you value: family, career, possessions, friends, hobbies, interests, likes and dislikes, attitudes, values, and whatever it is you consider your motivational, spiritual, or religious base. It includes everything you have experienced: childhood, school, good times, bad times, difficulty, pleasure, vacation, work, relationships. It includes everything you *want* to be a part of you in the future: goals, experiences, people.

Rule Two: Know and Appreciate Your Resource Inventory (RI)

All you have been and all you are—these are your resources. They have been shaped and reshaped through each experience in your life. Each will continue to be reshaped as you experience every new moment of life. The difference in how you used your RI in the past and how you will use it in the future will be how you look at each experience, how you fit it within a positive view of who you are and who you wish to be. Guided by these thoughts, you can be who you want to be—just add the ingredient of quality.

As we are shaped by our experiences and resources throughout our life, we shape our reality in the process. If this sounds vague, consider a concrete example. When I was young I created pictures with crayons. When I drew pictures of people, I could use the pink crayon labeled "flesh," or I could use the brown crayon or perhaps the black. I didn't think about it at the time, but these colors don't even vaguely resemble true skin tones. And only one, a dull pink crayon, was labeled "flesh." Yet those were my choices—my only available resources, if I wished to use crayons to make pictures. Life limited me and I didn't even know it. Fortunately, things change.

Rule Three: Open Your Mind to Options You Can't Currently Find

Today's kids are more richly blessed. The boxes of crayons they can use to draw people include a selection from among mahogany, peach, tan, sepia, burnt sienna, and apricot. It's a virtual multicultural rainbow of colors. The point is that today's young people have new and different resources available to them. The result is different products, different options, and different results—and ultimately, a different reality.

These new colors represent an expansion of the limits of reality. In fact, their very appearance in the crayon box means a host of new ideas, roads, and resources—what is real in the future. What does that mean for us? It means that each of us has within us the rainbow of colors—a series of untapped resources that can be called upon to generate different and new choices, options, and results. No one else can instill them; you must find them within yourself. They are there—waiting for you to trigger and use them. And you will, as long as you have the proper guidance.

Rule Four: Begin from the Vision

Let's begin by painting, with the colors of the rainbow, the vision you created in the previous chapter, using the resources you already have and those that lie within you.

EXERCISE: First, take a moment to review your vision for the future (and if you didn't think you really needed to write one out, then face the fact that you need to. Do it now).

For me, my vision is a career by which I will guide others on a journey inside themselves and along the road to previously untapped resources. One way to achieve this was writing a book.

You may wonder why I say *"begin* from the vision" when this beginning point doesn't come up until Rule Four. Good question, but I've found that many people can't get themselves to think about their vision until they have overcome all the negative blocks to growth— those things that stand in the way of creating a place in the mind where vision is important. If you don't appreciate your past, your current level of skills and your resources, and if your mind is closed to options, whether or not you can yet see them, then you aren't ready to think about vision. Eventually, Rules One to Three will have become so much a part of your thinking that you'll forget they even are rules. Then, vision will take over.

Go back to the concept of vision. What have you written down so far? Do you have scattered words, phrases, abstract concepts? Good. Right now, that's all you need. You may be moved to start jotting ideas about how you will live out your vision. Fine. Go ahead and do so, but don't confuse the plan and goals with the vision. Just keep the vision as short and energetic as possible—even if it seems broad. After all, there will be obstacles and forces in your path. But, you must always know where your rainbow awaits you.

One vision statement I heard the other day has stuck with me. "I am on this planet to give service." Sounds a bit vague. Yet this woman, now in her mid-70s, has always known that whatever she does in life can serve someone else, not just herself. She defines service very broadly—she didn't need this book to help her do that. As you will see later, we can all live our lives as if service was our goal.

This woman caught on to the concept of *quality* service. When she buys a dress she thinks—quite consciously—how she is serving the people who produced the material, cut the cloth, loaded it in a truck, sold it to her, and so forth. She is in a service business herself, and when she delivers her product she knows that she is one person in a chain of people who are ultimately benefiting others. It's a beautiful concept, actually.

We are all interdependent; our every action has the potential to be a service to others, from others, and for others. But we must guide and control that interaction between all parts to ensure quality—so others benefit from the quality you live.

EXERCISE: Now, take a moment to understand your basepoint. Take the next several minutes (as long as it takes) and write out a list of experiences, values, and those things you wish to be a part of your life in the future. Consider as you write each point which skill or skills you relied upon for each experience and value. Reflect upon what skills you needed but did not have available at the time.

EXERCISE: Next, look to your plans for the future and write out what specific skills and resources you will need to accomplish each thing.

If you're confused, think about it this way. Every day of your life has been an opportunity to live and experience life consciously. Some days you are quite aware of this, and other days you probably would just as soon forget. Recognize that you are shaping each tomorrow you live, based on, at least in part, what you learned yesterday and what you are learning today. In other words, a quality mind never damns the past. The past—all of it—has value in some way. Your experiences (the good and the bad), skills, successes, and non-successes are all available to serve you now. Will you throw them away, or will you use them?

As you move through this exercise, remember that each of us has created our own life through the resources we have been aware of around us as we grew up. For example, the person raised on a farm with a dozen siblings will not have the same experiences, attitudes, and beliefs as a person who was raised in a Manhattan high-rise as an only child. One is not better than the other; both lives were built on resources that were present at every moment of that life.

The most difficult experiences to explain are instances of abuse, the loss of loved ones, or a debilitating accident which renders a person disabled—both physically and likely, psychologically. How can such events be of value—they serve no positive purpose. It's true that these experiences in and of themselves are tragic, sometimes criminal, and never explicable. Those who commit wrongful acts to another must surely pay the consequences; those we lose must certainly be mourned, and tremendous adaptations need be made in the face of atrocity. For many people, years of therapy and counseling are a key to adaptation. In some cases, we can motivate and propel ourselves under our own force.

But what lasting impact will we accept in our life? Will we permit a troubled or tragic past to guide *us* to a life of wrong-doing or failure? Will we live in self pity or shame?

While certainly an option, the demands for a quality life would send us on another track. Take all the time necessary to uncover how you can and will grow stronger from such experiences. An abusive past can lead you to assist others and to make efforts to ensure that others do not experience what you endured. The loss of someone dear can empower us to live the values and dreams taught to us by that person, sharing them with others and ensuring that the person lives on in spirit and deed. The loss of physical function has propelled many to re-channel their lives and potential towards rights for the disabled—and enhanced research to make a seemingly hopeless task possible once again.

Each of us on this planet is presented with opportunity. It is our decision to use or forsake it, to forge ahead or lag behind, to accept (or live in denial with) a troubled past or to force ourselves onward—and upward.

The secret is to learn to work towards an acceptance of our past, to appreciate the differences among us and develop the quality of empathy in order to learn how these other people view life. Then their resources can become your resources and your overall ability to view life from the eyes of other people will sharpen. In other words, so much more lies inside, once we can locate it!

Think of the vision that can become reality once we tap into all we have within us—the internal power that comes from viewing "failures" as feedback for how *not* to do things. The potential is vast if you don't forget Rule One. Look with a positive eye towards your past and present. You see, we don't criticize Edison because he didn't invent the computer; we admire him for inventing the light bulb. In fact, Edison once said that his first thousand non-successes in inventing the light bulb weren't failures at all; they provided information about how the experiment would *not* work. Imagine if he took the first non-success as a sign to stop, or for that matter, the first ten, the first hundred, or first several hundred. You see, the answer was *always* there—Edison just needed to find it. He never failed; he just didn't know how to succeed, at least at first.

I once heard that George Washington Carver asked the peanut to reveal its secrets to him. He was sure that the peanut could be used in a host of ways that no one had thought of yet. So, as he used trial and error in his laboratory, he asked the peanut for its cooperation. It's as if he intuitively knew that the knowledge was there for the asking. Perhaps in this story there is the true meaning of the words, "Seek and ye shall find, knock and the door will be opened unto you." We don't find if we don't seek, and the good in life doesn't race around looking for us. We must act, and sometimes we won't get it right in the first effort. Does this require the intelligence and experience of being an adult? Fortunately, far from it.

If you think about it, no one in this world works harder than babies. In fact, no one learns more about non-successes than these little developing human beings. When a baby first learns to walk, he or she falls down over and over again. What if that baby gave up? What if a baby stopped reaching for a toy that is just an inch or two beyond its grasp? Eventually we all learned how to crawl because we wanted to grab for what was just out of reach.

As you can see, it isn't only well-known people who use the resources available to them. They just happen to be the ones we most often read about. You have always used what you have around you too, and your experiences provide the feedback you need to move forward. You just need to take control—that's what Carver, Edison, and all babies do. You may just have forgotten that you've done it, too.

Rule Five: Manage Your Life—Become Your Life's Worst S.O.B.

Many of the people in that hotel ballroom had forgotten that they weren't coming to a motivational seminar empty-handed. They were coming with a basepoint—skills and abilities, beliefs and attitudes, possessions, friends, and family. In short, these people brought their backgrounds, rich with resources, along with them. We often forget the resources we had and have available. We can become trapped in the past. Too many of us engage in an "all or nothing" phenomenon. Either we're on top of the world and invincible, or we say that nothing is working, and just maybe, nothing ever did.

We need to reverse our thinking a bit if we are going to bring about change in our less than perfect lot in life. Control begins when you begin to exert it.

Who makes the decisions in *your* life? Who influences you and your life? Whose lives do *you* influence? So where does the S.O.B. concept fit in?

Before you get the wrong idea, understand that being an S.O.B. does not mean making anyone's life miserable—including your own. It means making demands on your own life and establishing expectations for others who are part of your life, expectations that can be met. It means not being lax about what you can accomplish and what you do or can expect from others. For example, do you like to sleep late? Well, consider getting up early and accomplishing some tasks that never seem to get done. Do you bow to what others want you to do, even if it means falling a step back in your own goals? Well, consider exploring implications and consequences with these other people until a better and more self-aware resolution can be created.

Once again, start from where you are now. Have you engaged in all or nothing-at-all thinking? Ever? Yesterday? Today? Begin to catch yourself when you use universal phrases such as, "I always...," I never...," "It will never change...." Few experiences or values lack options or exceptions.

Realize too that implementing a new program is not something that is done in one big gulp, or one great sweeping motion. When companies begin quality programs, they start by taking small steps. They form their vision, explore the areas that need improvement, take the first step, and then take another. Management tries one strategy, checks out results, and moves on. If a manager said: "Well, that strategy was a failure. I guess we should chuck the whole program." most people would wonder how that person ever got to be a manager. Management of others and of our own life means having an overview and uncovering the steps to trigger personal growth.

When you plan your self-management program, think in terms of steps, small goals, little accomplishments. For example, you decide not to sleep late anymore. You're going to get up and work on your goal setting and planning. Will you do this every day? Why not start with Mondays and Fridays? What about changing what you do with your time one hour every other day?

Non-successes often happen when we expect ourselves to change everything—and all at one time. This is often the problem with typical motivational seminars, talks, and books. For some reason we come to believe we must change everything right *now.* The reality is that we are all human beings; we just can't do that.

All or nothing thinking has to change, and it will as you learn more about the quality mind-set and incorporate it in your day-to-day life. The quality movement in business could never have survived in an atmosphere of negative thinking. In fact, the principles which underlie the quality movement preclude this attitude from playing a role in your life. Quality thinking and quality living are based on constant evaluation and slow, steady change.

Rule Six: Demanding Quality of Yourself and Others

Do you approach motivation or your potential for growth from a position of strength or from weakness? Do you give yourself credit for what you already know, already have, and have already accomplished?

Take a few moments to experience your "Quality Quotient"—that is, the extent to which you are open to (and have the ability to demand) quality in your life. You won't be giving yourself a grade here, nor will you compare yourself with other people. Just get a sense of your current basepoint from the quality perspective. Once you take the measure, you will have a better sense of what direction you wish to go, how much work is ahead, and how much faith you currently have in your ability to make a change.

The Quality Quotient

Rate yourself on each of the following questions by circling the number closest to your response.

1. How do you view past non-successes? Are they failures in your life, or do you consider them to be feedback for the future? Are some experiences failures and others learning?

    ____1_____2_____3_____4_____5_____6_____7____
    FAILURE   **FEEDBACK**

2. Define your view of a life purpose up to this moment. Take a few minutes and think about the way you've lived. Does life just happen to you, or do you guide and control your own life?

    ____1_____2_____3_____4_____5_____6_____7____
    LIFE HAPPENS TO ME   **I GUIDE MY LIFE**

    If you haven't guided your life, try to write out the principles that you would like to guide you as you move through life, beginning today.

3. Think about the skills you believe are the most important assets in both your professional and personal life. Do you believe that life's skills are learned formally in school or are innate? For exam-

_____	**Neuro-Linguistic Programming**........................	$24.00
	Dilts, Grinder, Bandler et al Limited Edition (hardcover)	
_____	**The Elusive Obvious**.............................	$20.00
	Moshe Feldenkrais (hardcover)	
_____	**Patterns of Hypnotic Techniques of Milton H. Erickson, M.D. – Volume I**...............	$17.95
	Bandler and Grinder (paper)	
_____	**Patterns of Hypnotic Techniques of Milton H. Erickson, M.D. – Volume II**...............	$19.95
	Bandler, DeLozier, Grinder (hardcover)	
_____	**Provocative Therapy**.............................	$15.95
	Farrelly & Brandsma (hardcover)	
_____	**Practical Magic**................................	$15.95
	Stephen R. Lankton (paper)	
_____	**Therapeutic Metaphors**	$15.95
	David Gordon (paper)	

ORDER FORM   FAX WITH MASTERCARD/VISA OR MAIL THIS CARD TO:

Meta Publications Inc.
P. 0. Box 1910, Capitola, CA 95010
(408) 464-0254 Fax (408) 464-0517

Please send me copies of the books ordered

Subtotal

Tax (add 8% for California residents)

Freight & Handling (U.S.A. only)   4.00

TOTAL AMOUNT ENCLOSED $ _____

☐ Check here for complete catalog

Name_____

Address_____

City_____ State _____ Zip _____

Charge to my credit card: ☐ Visa   ☐ MasterCard

  #_____ Exp. Date _____

Signature _____
    (Credit Card Only)

BOOK LIST

Quantity

_____	**Quality Mind, Quality Life**............................	$19.95
	Paul Lisnek (hardcover)	
_____	**Effective Presentation Skills**..........................	$22.95
	Robert Dilts (hardcover)	
_____	**Time for a Change**..................................	$19.95
	Richard Bandler (hardcover)	
_____	**Skills for the Future**	$27.95
	Robert Dilts (hardcover)	
_____	**Magic in Action – Revised**	$19.95
	Richard Bandler (hardcover)	
_____	**The Adventures of Anybody**.........................	$12.95
	Richard Bandler (hardcover)	
_____	**Tools for Dreamers**	$27.95
	Dilts , Epstien & Dilts (hardcover)	
_____	**Changing Belief Systems with NLP**....................	$22.00
	Robert Dilts (hardcover)	
_____	**No Experience Necessary**	$12.95
	Scott Nelson (paper)	
_____	**Beyond Selling**....................................	$19.95
	Dan S. Bagley & Edward J. Reese (hardcover)	
_____	**Time Line Therapy**.................................	$22.95
	Tad James & Wyatt Woodsmall (hardcover)	
_____	**The Magic of Rapport**..............................	$14.95
	Jerry Richardson (paper)	
_____	**An Insider's Guide To Submodalities**	$12.95
	Richard Bandler & Will MacDonald (paper)	
_____	**The Master Moves**.................................	$14.95
	Moshe Feldenkrais (paper)	
_____	**Roots of Neuro-Linguistic Programming**	$22.00
	Robert Dilts (hardcover)	
_____	**Applications of Neuro-Linguistic Programming**..........	$22.00
	Robert Dilts (hardcover)	
_____	**Meta-Cation: Prescriptions for Some Ailing Educational Processes**........................	$12.00
	Sid Jacobson (hardcover)	
_____	**Phoenix—Therapeutic Patterns of Milton H. Erickson**....	$15.95
	D. Gordon & M. Myers-Anderson (paper)	

(See other side for more books and order form.)

ple, which skills were developed by observing other people such as your parents and which have you always seemed to have available to you?

____1_____2_____3_____4_____5_____6_____7____

SKILLS ARE INNATE   **SKILLS ARE LEARNED**

Take a moment to write out the skills you have learned and those you always seemed to have available to you, and draft some situations in which you use these various skills. Use this exercise to begin expanding your existing skills as well as exploring your untapped human resources.

4. Are there activities or skills you believe you do particularly well, perhaps even better than most people you know?

____1_____2_____3_____4_____5_____6_____7____

FEW SKILLS BETTER THAN MOST   **MANY BETTER THAN MOST**

What are these skills?

5a. Are there shortcomings that seem to hold you back, preventing you from achieving your goals?

____1_____2_____3_____4_____5_____6_____7____

SEVERAL SHORTCOMINGS   **FEW SHORTCOMINGS**

5b. How important are they to your success?

____1_____2_____3_____4_____5_____6_____7____

IMPORTANT TO MY SUCCESS   **NOT IMPORTANT TO SUCCESS**

6. Do you use your assets and strengths to their full advantage in your life? Do you have skills that appear to be going to waste?

____1_____2_____3_____4_____5_____6_____7____

WASTING SKILLS   **UTILIZING SKILLS**

---

7. Do you effectively use family, friends, work associates, and other people who are part of your life to provide you with those skills you don't currently possess? Or do you rely solely on your own skills, leaving whatever you are unable to do to remain undone?

____1_____2_____3_____4_____5_____6_____7____
RELY ON THE SELF   **UTILIZE OTHERS**

Remember that people are important resources to you. Take a moment to list all the human resources you have at your disposal. How do these people help you?

8a. Do you demand excellence in your own life—from yourself?

____1_____2_____3_____4_____5_____6_____7____
DON'T DEMAND EXCELLENCE   **STRONGLY DEMAND**

8b. Do you demand it from others?

____1_____2_____3_____4_____5_____6_____7____
DON'T DEMAND EXCELLENCE   **STRONGLY DEMAND**

9. Consider how you define excellence. What does demanding excellence require? Do you see this as a challenge?

____1_____2_____3_____4_____5_____6_____7____
TOO DIFFICULT TO DEMAND   **WELCOME CHALLENGE**

10. Do you see life mostly as full of challenges or mostly as full of problems?

____1_____2_____3_____4_____5_____6_____7____
PROBLEMS   **CHALLENGES**

11. Do you view the people in your life as obstacles or assets?

____1_____2_____3_____4_____5_____6_____7____
OBSTACLES   **ASSETS**

Which people in your life fall into each category? You might as well be honest, because you can't work on change for the future if you aren't honest about the present. Take a moment or two to write down your human resource list.

12. Is your life a series of reactions or a series of actions? Think about this carefully. It may contain an important principle that has knowingly or unknowingly guided your life.

____1_____2_____3_____4_____5_____6_____7____
REACTIONS   **ACTIONS**

13. Imagine we meet on the street and I ask you what your vision is for the next year, five years, and ten years. Do you scoff at the question? Do you welcome the inquiry? Take a minute to think about why you answered the way you did.

____1_____2_____3_____4_____5_____6_____7____
SCOFF AT THE INQUIRY   **WELCOME**

14. Do you fear or welcome the future? Do you believe that you can plan for its arrival?

____1_____2_____3_____4_____5_____6_____7____
FEAR   **WELCOME**

You are probably wondering if you've passed or failed this test. I believe that you, as a person who obviously wants to take charge of your life, are smart enough to figure out where you stand on the various questions. I hope you will take some time to explore why you answered each question the way you did. Think how much more valuable this list of questions will be if you go back to them numerous times and monitor how your attitudes change over time.

Now, take a moment to add up your score from the above questions and compare your score to the following scale. This is a guide. If you scored between:

15 and 25, you are controlled by circumstances and do not exert control over your own life.

26 and 45, you are more controlled by outside factors than you control them. Evaluating and setting priorities will be necessary to regain control over those areas of life which are important to your success.

46 and 75, you are able to control some facets of your life, but are controlled by others in some areas. The question becomes which decisions and areas of your life you are not controlling that you need to control, and which decisions and areas you control that may or may not be important for your success.

76 and 90, you control most decisions and resources in your life, but there is room for improvement. Our lives are controlled by many factors and we need significant control over as many components as possible.

91 and 98, you are in great control over your own life. You use the resources available to you to their fullest and know how to integrate other people into your own vision and goals.

Once you have reviewed your score or "Quality Quotient" and its interpretation, give some thought to the following questions as the first step at strengthening your control over the many facets of your life:

What attitudes and values are most important to you? Which are not as important? How do these attitudes and values get expressed in your life? What do you want more of? Perhaps just as important, what do you wish to have less of in your life?

You may notice that some of your beliefs and ways of thinking have changed over the past few years. I've heard many people say that they used to approach the future with great hope and optimism, but that as they grew older, their attitude subtly changed. Now they are more fearful, less willing to take risks. But, they *can* have the adventurous and optimistic attitude they once held dear. In this case, people need to look at resources they have misplaced or permitted to rest dormant, not resources they never had in the first place.

This is likely to be a valuable time for you to take a few minutes and review for yourself what you want to get from reading this book. Why did you buy it? What did you hope to gain? Why did the concept of quality appeal to you? Are you prepared to accept the challenge of making changes in your life? Can you accept your answers as the first step of opportunity to create change and gain control in your own life?

When you measured your Quality Quotient, you began the process of examining your own quality base and awareness of your Resource Inventory. Along with the vision you wrote in the first chapter, this is the beginning of your understanding of a quality mind approach. You must remember that you begin this opportunity from a position of strength, your basepoint. Don't forget about all the resources you already have in your life.

Like the people at the seminar I described earlier, we often look for a new start, a new path, rather than building on what we already have available and have already accomplished. Value your resources; give yourself credit for them. If your life is filled with supportive friends and a loving family, remember that you created that support. It didn't just happen. It happened because of the kind of person you are and the way you use your resources. If you are less than satisfied with the quality level in your life, then relax, the change has already begun.

You have already used many key operating skills to create the life you presently live. No matter how slight or underdeveloped these skills may appear to you right now, they are inside your storehouse of resources. These resources will help you begin your quest for a quality life, which in turn, will prod you on to find or create other resources. For now, affirm in your own mind that you have a goal to get in touch with these resources and that you will channel them toward the successful life you want. Begin by bringing peace to that internal critic inside us all—that part of us that gets in the way of progress and growth.

Silencing the Critic

Many people are far too hard on themselves. We have this internal "critic," whose job seems to be to tell us never to be satisfied with anything. This is the voice that tells us that what we do isn't good enough, and it tries to discourage us whenever we seek change. This inner critic tends to dismiss everything and everybody that takes us up the ladder of life.

Did you ever hear someone exclaim: "I hate my job and I never should have taken it in the first place!"? When I hear a statement like that I always probe a bit deeper. "How did you feel when you were offered that job?" I'll ask. Nine times out of ten, the person will say, "Oh, at the time, it was great! I'd been through three interviews and I was offered more money than I'd been making on my other job. It seemed like a great opportunity, a fresh start." These people look positively nostalgic as they reflect and talk about this experience.

How can this be the same person who was so certain the decision to take the job had been the right one at the time? The person's personal "backyard," once filled with flowers, has become overgrown with weeds, usually because it was neglected, not cultivated. The original splendor of the garden is all but forgotten, thanks to the efforts of the internal critic. The quality movement in the business world and a quality mind do not pay attention to the simplistic and harmful voice of the critic.

Appreciating your current skills is extremely important when you are deciding where you want to go, what you want to be, and the future you want to create. By evaluating your current and past circumstances and identifying your skills and strengths, you are far more likely to approach the future with confidence and zest. People who believe life doesn't work and never did, will find the process of change and development too overwhelming to begin. These people remain stuck.

Look at it this way: it is easier to climb higher when you're already on the ladder. If you're stuck in a place where you're cursing the ladder, progress isn't likely. So, develop a sense of where you are on the quality ladder of life. Remember, even if you are on a lower rung, you *are* on the ladder already! Let's begin our climb.

Taking Quality Thinking into Your Life: Nine to Five

I find that the majority of people who decide to create change in their lives often identify their career as a focus for that change. In fact, because we spend so much of our time working, we often sense the first glimmers of our dissatisfaction with life when we notice that we don't look forward to going to work. We end up dreading the day ahead, get caught up in office gossip, or find that we are tired, bone-tired, when we go home. In short, the zest is gone.

People who view their work as play leave their jobs invigorated and happy. Fatigue that comes from enjoyable, challenging work is good fatigue. Ever have the *good* kind of job? Think about it. Do you know the difference between "good tired" and "bad tired"?

Unfortunately, rather than examining the reasons for this dissatisfaction, we might think, "This job was a disaster from day one." We may even feel guilty. After all, our neighbor doesn't even have a job and our sister-in-law just learned her company is being sold. Consequently, we add to our discomfort by feeling guilty about our attitude. This might cause us to stay quiet, thereby cutting off opportunities to use the resources around us—our family and friends, for example. So, we go on hating our job and feeling guilty about it to boot.

If we trace this process back to its roots, the trouble did not begin when we realized that we no longer looked forward to going to the office or factory. It began when we told ourselves that the whole experience was bad from the start. In fact, I would wager that at least 90 percent of us enjoy every job we have when we first start it. (There's always the 10 percent for whom the fit *was* wrong from day one.) After all, every new job is usually filled with challenges and new skills to learn. Maybe we are promoted after a time, and this presents us with still more variety. Our co-workers may be pleasant most of the time, and we even get along with the boss. If we are enjoying ourselves and accepting challenges and the growth they trigger, then we are likely using our available resources; we are guiding the process of creating a satisfying career.

Sooner or later, however, the challenges are met, the new opportunities for growth begin to be chipped away, and we may wake up one day and realize that we haven't had a promotion for quite a while. On the surface, it would seem that developing a case of job "blahs" is a perfectly normal response. A friend of mine had the job blahs for almost 10 years before he made a move on his own behalf. When I asked him about it, he said that he stayed so long that he began to think of the blahs as normal—he'd forgotten that he could be happy on a job.

What would happen if, instead of concluding that everything is terrible, we said, "The challenge is finished here, so I must have learned about all I can. I wonder what I should do next?" What if we were to say, "I'm glad I had the opportunity to learn all these skills at this job because they will help with the next challenge I decide to take on." Or, we can say, "Maybe I shouldn't get another job; maybe I should start a business, or go back to school. What do I really want to do with my life right now?" These attitudes promote our well-being and self-esteem. They also promote the process of engagement—listening to ourselves and asking questions for us to consider. This is the process of feedback in action; thoughts of failure don't even enter the picture.

When we find ourselves asking the questions, feeling the blahs, or wondering what went "wrong," it's time to go back to our vision. This is the time to say, "I'll look at what is presently going on with my career, and I'll see where it fits, or doesn't fit with my vision. Maybe my job can no longer serve my vision. So, what will serve it? What will carry it forth?" It is amazing how much energy is sparked when we use vision as our gauge, or touchstone—the tool with which we evaluate what is going on in the present moment.

Danielle was recently laid off from a well-paying job as an accountant in a large corporation began to look for a new position similar to the one she'd had. At first, she never considered doing anything else but finding another job. But, she began to notice the lack of enthusiasm she managed to muster for the interviews she had. Not surprisingly, she wasn't offered those jobs. I imagine her lack of energy and enthusiasm for the positions came through in her interviews. She took a week or two off from her job search and spent her time puttering around in her apartment, taking long walks, and talking with friends.

By the end of the two weeks, Danielle knew that she had no desire to go back into her original field. "If I don't want to be an accountant anymore," she asked herself, "what do I want to do?" Fortunately, this woman was able to silence her inner critic who tried to urge her to accept any job just to have one. She was able to engage in a month of exploration and soul searching, with reflection on the skills and resources she had used in that work setting. Reflecting on her vision and her available resources taught her that what she needed to do was work for herself.

From that point on, Danielle's energy returned and she was able to make the necessary plans to accomplish her goal. Of course, this didn't happen overnight. She ended up taking a part-time accounting job while she explored a world of new options that were now blossoming in her mind. Today, she owns half interest in a cafe, and she works independently with a few clients who use her accounting services.

It should be obvious that Danielle did not engage in all-or-nothing thinking. For example, just because she decided that she no longer wanted to be an accountant, she didn't toss the career out the window. No, she used that skill to support herself while she opened up the new doors upon which she chose to knock. She was able to combine and integrate her resources, not throw them out.

Danielle listened to the dissatisfied voice inside herself without letting the critic take over. We can all practice this process of engaging with ourselves and realizing the power we have over our lives. We don't need to believe that staying in the same job or the same profession is simply fate—that because we are there now, it must always be. Change can be self-initiated.

The more we engage in the process of self-examination, and the more we are able to silence the critic, the less likely we are to believe that things just happen to us randomly. We need to focus on the skills and resources that drive us in a particular setting and explore how they can be useful in other settings as we grow and progress professionally through life.

Quality living means using all the resources you've just examined, and exploring your skills—those I call key operating skills. The next chapters of the book will integrate resources and skills in each phase of your life: work, personal issues, and social activities.

For example, when you hear the word "negotiation," what comes to your mind? Labor unions or legal settlements? Buying a home or car? Working out contract terms? Bring your current negotiating skills with you when you begin to learn more about quality thinking in the work environment. Some people might say, "But I don't have any skills like that. I've never negotiated anything in my life."

My approach to change recognizes you *have* negotiated at some point in your life. If you are over the age of three, you have negotiated something. If you have another person living with you who is over the age of three, chances are you have negotiated a lot. From our earliest conversations, we negotiate "deals." We negotiate when we want a toy, a meal, and as we get older, where we will eat, whether to be on time for school, where to go to college, while returning a defective product, getting out of a traffic ticket, and on and on. We go through the give and take process throughout life and this process is all negotiation.

Right now, think of all the things you do during the course of your day that require you to give and take, demand and compromise. Perhaps you do not think you do this "well enough." Don't judge for now. Just be aware that you used whatever skills you had to put the deal together. Placed in this context, you will have a new awareness helping you to enhance your own skills, sharpen them, and view them as necessary to the pursuit of a chosen life. But, if you take a few minutes right now and give yourself credit for what you have already accomplished in this arena, then you will get more from that chapter and the entire book.

Our work life also requires the ability to create organization in whatever tasks we must, or choose, to pursue. Clearly, this skill is essential in every part of our life, but we must begin by taking stock where the skills are of significant and daily import. Do you believe you are unorganized? Most people believe that they have room for improvement in this area. That's fine. There is usually room for improvement in many areas of life. But, if you've ever written a paper, changed a diaper, drafted a check, read a train schedule, driven a car, or replaced a battery in a radio, you have used organizational skills. As the projects we are involved with become more complex, we become conscious that we are using a special set of skills that require logical thinking and a methodology.

After Five: Quality in Relationships

Communication may be the most important skill available to you in every setting, but it becomes highlighted in an analysis of our interpersonal relationships. Most often, our relations with a spouse, lover, parent, sibling, or child, all develop blocks as a result of communication barriers. You may or may not believe that you communicate well, but be assured that by the time you finish examining your communication skills in interpersonal relationships, you will have a foundation from which to take your communication skills into many arenas and to watch your relationships grow in every setting.

Think about how much your relationships affect your success in every facet of your life.

Do you have trouble concentrating at work because of unresolved issues at home? Are you frustrated that you can't get through to your children or significant other? Relationships are complicated. We may assume too much skill on our part. Because we spend so much time interacting with others, we assume we do it well.

Growth begins first from a recognition that we have room to improve. Your Quality Quotient has likely already pointed out room for growth. Work in the area of interpersonal relationships will spill over to every other part of your life.

Remember, you don't start from square one on your ability to communicate. If you are a functioning adult, you have communicated—maybe even well sometimes, and, because you're human, you may not have communicated in the way you would have liked. Consider your experiences as feedback, rather than failures. As you examine your communication skills, don't be judgmental, be creative. Consider all the ways you communicate both verbally and non-verbally with others.

Examine your communications over the last several days. Did you ask for help from someone in a store? Did you talk to your spouse about a problem? Did you discuss a new project with a coworker? Perhaps you had an argument with someone. How did you feel about the result? What could you have done better?

You'll learn techniques that you can put to use immediately that will enhance your existing communication skills. Your new knowledge will take you several rungs higher on your ladder of a quality life and create new possibilities for you to expand and prosper in your social networks.

The Whole is Greater Than the Sum of its Parts: Social Network

Interpersonal relationships are the groundwork for social interactions. Success at social gatherings can translate to increased business and networking. Being in a social interaction means monitoring the different parts of our being and calling upon those skills needed as we interact with different people. Managing people is not an easy task, so conflict should be a commonly anticipated occurrence.

The good news is that conflict, often seen as problematic and a threat to social networks, is actually a positive force. Conflict can be good if it is managed effectively. Conflict management and resolution skills become the focus for handling our network of social interactions. Keeping peace with a multitude of people with whom we interact, whether by choice or necessity, is an essential skill to overall growth and nurturing of our relationships.

You will come to see your social relationships as a "life team." Building your personal team will be fundamental to your overall success in managing all kinds of relationships and your life.

Remember the quality movement's goal in business of zero defects? I talked about this with a group of friends who, expressing enormous discomfort, said that it sounded as if we could become machines, perfect technocrats, operating like robots, never making a mistake. Permit a redefinition of zero defects as applied to a quality mind and a quality life. For example, if we eliminate waste, overcome obstacles, and refuse to engage in all or nothing thinking, then we are on the way to zero defects. Let's look at the concept of zero defects as gradually eliminating what we don't want or need in our lives and replacing it with more of what we do want or need.

Let's use our vision to help us see if we are moving toward or away from a take charge attitude. Are we hanging on to houses, jobs, relationships, or other things that no longer serve our vision? Or, are we gradually changing internally and externally? Keep in mind that your goal is not to reach perfection. You see, a drive towards perfection in ourselves is engaging in all or nothing thinking. That's not what we're about.

Making it All Happen

Creating a vision, knowing and developing the resources and skills that accompany it, and developing a quality mind attitude are all well and good, but they don't insure success. The underlying concern in every situation and each relationship is being able to decide when and how to use quality thinking and how to judge the factors that play a role in each decision situation.

74

When you make a decision, do you believe that you are using a skill? It may surprise you to know that many people do not view decision-making as a skill at all. They believe it just happens, that they think about something for a while and then a decision just happens. Some decisions are difficult, some are easy, but somehow they just happen. Wrong—a decision never just happens. A decision is a result of conscious and unconscious processes, and a complex interaction between them, your intellect, and your emotions. Sometimes we barely notice the process; at other times, formulating a decision seems like pure agony.

Fortunately, like all the other skills discussed in each specific part of our life, you already have a lot of practice making decisions. You may even consider yourself a decisive person. If so, good. The chapter on decision-making will help you become even better at it. If you perceive yourself as indecisive, or maybe even wishy-washy, then decision-making skills may be the most important skills you sharpen by reading this book. Communication, negotiation, and conflict resolution can all be improved and learned, but they don't operate effectively in the life vision if decisions regarding their use are not properly thought out.

A quality mind–quality life program starts with making small decisions day by day until you gain confidence in this skill. Then each resource and skill is evaluated properly in context. You will see every facet of the quality approach becoming more clear and more easily implemented in your life.

One incident at the large seminar I attended illustrates this marvelous phenomenon of proper decision-making and stands out more than any other.

A young couple had come from Minneapolis, driving all day, to hear this famous motivational speaker, and their present circumstances were, frankly, not very good. I happened to sit next to them just before the program began.

Sandy had recently lost her job because the company she worked for had packed up and moved to Mexico. Ray, her husband of seven years, had been out of work for eleven months. He was doing repair jobs for neighbors, sending resumes out by the dozens, and attempting to maintain a cheerful attitude. Sandy believed they needed a radical change. She was sure that they were stuck in old patterns and were living life based on old expectations. They had no clue as to how to begin the decision-making process, much less knowing what skills they could call upon to assist them.

I took an immediate liking to this attractive, friendly couple, both in their 30s and showing an eager and obvious enthusiasm for each other and, despite their problems, for life itself. I thought that Ray was remarkably resourceful in using the few tools he owned to make some money while also methodically going about the business of finding a new sales job. His cheerful, trusting attitude about life nicely complemented Sandy's conviction that perhaps she and Ray needed to look at more than the "help wanted" pages.

I liked the way Sandy was willing to examine her attitudes and attempt to break patterns. As she put it, "Ray and I were both raised to think that our jobs were our security. We didn't rock the boat and we never thought about doing anything else but just get another job, almost any job would do. It's the way our parents lived their lives. But the industries in our city were stable for years. The world has changed, and we can't keep doing the same old things. Maybe we should move, go back to school, or do something really different—I don't even know what."

Even though he displayed a positive attitude now, Ray had not been particularly enthusiastic about coming to this seminar. Ray was there because he had gone along with Sandy's desire to attend. Ray, like many people, thought that change was possible in good times, but once the hard days set in, it was better to do the expected and the predictable. Planning for a major change in direction just didn't seem possible. "I think we need to stabilize things first," he said. "Then we can reevaluate." There was no vision, and no thought about available resources and skills.

During one of the breaks about halfway through the program, this affable couple were having a polite, but obvious, disagreement. Sandy was quite fired up about the program, and she was ready to sign up for a lengthier, intensive seminar. She was sure that it would change her life—and therefore, their lives. Unfortunately, the fee for the more intensive seminar would use up just about all the savings they had left. Ray just couldn't see risking the money. There was no way he could justify wiping out their savings when within a month or two they might need it simply to pay for basics such as rent and food.

It became quite clear to all of us who were standing with them that Ray and Sandy were used to negotiating their way through these kinds of problems. However, they both threw up their hands and told the rest of us that they had reached an impasse. I wasn't surprised. They had no rationale for exploring or reaching a decision.

There is probably nothing more fascinating than the trusting behavior that can result when a group of strangers form a temporary bond. The five or six people—including me—who had become part of Ray and Sandy's "basepoint," at least for the moment, threw caution to the wind and got involved in their discussion. (This is usually a bad move unless one is specifically invited, so I'm not recommending it. But in this setting it seemed quite appropriate.) Under other circumstances, Ray and Sandy might have told us to "butt out." However, the tone of the seminar had been upbeat and there was exciting energy in the room. In addition, we had gained a genuine desire to help them solve their problem and they seemed to recognize our goodwill.

My legal mind couldn't resist trying to find a solution—preferably one that would be satisfying to both Sandy and Ray. In an informal way, I moderated the process and suggested a rational approach for walking through the decision-making process, a process I will share with you later in this book. First, the other half dozen people threw out suggestions and I kept track of them. I asked Sandy and Ray to listen to all the ideas before they judged any of them. They were surprised by the interest in their dilemma, but they also seemed touched by it, and they cheerfully agreed to go along with my suggestions.

Ten minutes later a solution resulted, and perhaps even more important, the process was unforgettable. Though they didn't know it, the process was also structured and guided. It was unlikely that they could go wrong because they reflected on their vision, considered their resources, and looked at what else would be needed to create a solution.

Because we had agreed that no idea could be censored or rejected, people were quite creative. Ideas breed ideas, and within minutes, the people in our ad hoc group had suggested, among other things, that:

1) Sandy take the money but write out a plan specifying how she would replace it within 60 days;

2) Ray and Sandy borrow the money from their parents and both attend the weekend seminar;

3) they forget the whole thing (meaning that Sandy would have to abandon her desire);

4) Ray should give in and not worry about the consequences (meaning that he'd have to live with the anxiety about spending their savings);

5) Sandy should buy the tape series based on the long seminar, but for a fraction of the cost;

6) Sandy should buy the tape series and a selection of the training books available now, with Ray committing to look at the seminar idea again in six months.

Notice all the "crayons" that had always been available, but that neither Sandy nor Ray could "pull from the box." I was particularly gratified at how easily items five and six were combined, because it seemed to me that these were the viable solutions. Sandy, reluctantly at first, agreed to limit herself to the tapes and the books. Because Sandy had dropped the seminar idea for the moment, Ray promised her that they would look at it again in six months. He was open to the possibility that their circumstances—their available resources— would have changed. So, because Ray had been sincere about that, Sandy agreed to limit her purchases to the tapes and one book.

By the time the decision was reached, the whole group was smiling and laughing with delight. I believe it did us all good to see two people work their way through a situation, which, let's face it, could have ended up very ugly. Ray could have been made to feel like an authoritarian who was withholding something from his wife. Or, he could have lived with the anxiety over not having the money. Sandy might have ended up feeling deprived and hostile. She could have gone ahead and taken the money, knowing that Ray didn't like it, but she wouldn't have been happy about it.

Instead, a decision was reached using available resources—the backyard that already existed. Sandy didn't go to the seminar, but she was able to make a smaller investment in tapes and a book and still get some of the benefits. There was a realization that the process of change could begin from the place they presently occupied. Ray and Sandy's backyard included many things—old tapes about jobs and security that needed to be examined, and a recognition on Sandy's part that times were changing and she and Ray would need to adjust their actions accordingly. Of course, their backyard included many other things, not the least of which was the strong bond between them that enabled them to have a disagreement and work through it.

The resources available to Sandy and Ray included their past experiences and all the skills and abilities they accumulated in their three-plus decades on the planet. This interaction involved negotiation, communication, conflict management, and all of these within the structure of effective decision-making. More time would have permitted reflection about other resources they had individually and between them.

If I'd had more time with Sandy and Ray, I might have asked them about their vision. Did they each have an individual vision? Did they have a mission as a couple? What were their deepest desires—not in terms of lists of things, experiences, or accomplishments—but in terms of quality? Did they want to create more prosperity in their lives, more rewarding and pleasant careers, deeper more meaningful family relationships, closer bonds within their community, more time together committed just to play and laughter, more vitality in their day-to-day lives?

It is easy to see why they became confused over the decision about the seminar, not that it didn't turn out just fine. However, if they'd had the vision, the decision might have been easier. In truth, they might have easily come up with the "delayed gratification" solution much sooner. Ray would have seen the longer, more expensive seminar as a logical step in living Sandy's vision—or their own joint mission. Sandy would have seen that the resources weren't available and perhaps have come upon the compromise immediately.

Putting Quality Thinking to Work

It's easy to see how overwhelming the process of change can be if we indulge in the "life doesn't work and never has" or, "my job was wrong from the start" or, "my relationships have always been terrible" mentality. No wonder so many people rush to attend seminars, which, they believe, will transform them overnight. They are soon disappointed when they see that no one has yet come up with a reliable method for instantaneous change. The encouraging reality is that the most motivated among us have "off days;" the most skilled and able people have crises of confidence. The most successful person we know is still a human being and will never be perfect. The same is true for each of us.

So what are the requisite steps to creating a quality life?

1. Create a Vision—simple, direct, and comprehensive: the road that you are committed to travel, regardless of what path you may ultimately take to get there.

2. Create your Resource Inventory. Understand your available resources and identify those resources you need to achieve your vision. Together, your available and identified (whether or not currently available) resources will be the tools that will take you to your vision.

3. Identify the part of your life you wish to address—work, social, or personal. Each part of our life is connected and interdependent with the others, but we can only fix one world at a time.

4. Identify what is working well in your life and evaluate those areas that need to be changed. We'll be relying on what is working as a resource to address what still needs improvement or even major change.

5. Create a manageable goal or end that you will be committed to achieve. Remember, you can't change your whole life overnight, but you can take small steps each day towards that major change.

At this point, you will need to rely on the foundation skills, such as negotiation, decision-making, communication, and organization that will be addressed in the following chapters. As you read on, keep in mind those people whose success you admire and whose overall outlook on life seems positive and happy. You will see that they rarely dismiss any experience, any relationship, or any job as useless, bad from the start, or an entrapment. What you will find if you study successful people carefully is that they know why they had a particular job, why they needed to learn important lessons from a failed relationship, and what the peaks and valleys of their social networks have contributed to their lives. They are guided by the "everything has its purpose" philosophy, and success emerges in their lives.

Successful, happy people "show up for life," as the old saying goes. These people look at the resources they had in the past, and they evaluate their experiences and resources based on what was available to them. They look at their present circumstances in the same way. Successful people start from where they are right now; they dream their dreams and formulate their goals and pursue them through a guiding vision.

The successful people you admire represent a quality mind in action. Without realizing it, they activated the principles of the best of the human potential movement and the quality movement in business. When you begin to use these ideas to create the new and the different, you begin from a position of strength, not from scratch. In the next chapter, we'll look at the ways quality thinking works when the concepts and principles are pulled together. You will soon be on your way to a more fruitful professional and personal life.

CHAPTER IV

Putting it all Together

"I'VE GOT THIS GREAT PLAN NOW," Jim says to his friend, Sally, over lunch at the office cafeteria. "I believe my life will really change. I know I can do it."

"What's different?" his friend Sally asks. "How are you going to change?"

"Well," says Jim, "I'm starting my new plan by getting up every day at 5:00 am.—I've been wasting too much time sleeping. Three days a week, I'll work out on my treadmill for an hour, and the other two days, I'm going to work on my novel."

"I didn't know you were writing a novel," Sally says, amazed by the enthusiasm in her friend.

"Oh, I'm not working on it yet. I'm just getting started. Anyway, I'm also signing up for graduate school—then I can get a better job or at least a promotion here. That will start in the fall, but I've got to get ready for the exams. And then, I've decided that my apartment is too small, so I'm going to spend a couple of evenings a week looking for a new one. Last week, I signed up for an investment class—that's on Wednesdays. And since my divorce, I haven't been doing any dating. But now, I'm sure that I'll meet women and date on the weekends. I answered two personal ads yesterday."

"When will you sleep, Jim? You sound so busy I can't keep track of what you're going to do. It sounds exhausting."

"Oh, it will all work. I went to this seminar last weekend, and I've never been so motivated."

"Best of luck—and keep me posted. I'll be eager to know how it all turns out."

Jim began his new life with determination and enthusiasm, a list of things he wanted, and the resolve to get started right away. It all looked so good—so possible—on paper.

About two weeks later, Jim came to work looking pretty beat. Sally, sensing his fatigue, invited him to join her for lunch. It didn't take long for Jim to tell his tale of broken promises to himself.

"This morning was supposed to be the time I worked on the novel. But I've been blocked and just couldn't seem to get out of bed, much less start writing. I reset the alarm for 6:30, but I hated myself for doing it. The investment class ran late and I wanted to have coffee with a woman I met there. That ran late too—she was really interesting—so here I am today, exhausted."

"Oh, well. It's just one morning," Sally said in an encouraging tone.

"If that were true, I wouldn't be worried, but I can't seem to find time to look for an apartment and graduate school seems like a distant memory. I'm not sure what happened. I was so motivated a couple of weeks ago. Now it seems to have fallen apart. Oh well, I guess I just can't change—I'm too old and I've been this way too long."

"Oh, I'm not sure that's true," Sally said. "You're already a great guy, but maybe you tried to do too much."

Jim's Unfortunate Adventure

What happened to Jim is typical of many people who commit themselves to making changes in their lives. I don't know whether it's the fault of our culture, motivational seminars, or the general climate in which we live, but so many people believe that everything must be done *now*. Of course, procrastination often does stand in the way of accomplishment. When we can control our time and better negotiate our circumstances, then we can begin to tackle our priorities now, not later, not tomorrow, not next month. So we try, and if we take all this advice too literally, we fail.

Before you move on to the section of this book in which you will be helped to enhance the specific skills you need to achieve a quality life, it's important that you get into the most productive mind-set possible. And what is a productive mind-set? Was Jim's mind-set the most advantageous? He believed he failed because he couldn't get it right, couldn't quite pull it all together.

However, in the final analysis, Jim hadn't failed at all. If he had been open to it, he would have realized that he'd learned one of life's most valuable lessons—that real change comes slowly, generally one step at a time, and usually in individual areas of life we are working to improve—one at a time. In fact, if Jim had used his experience, not as failure, but as feedback to learn what *wasn't* working, he would have maintained the perspective that is so important to personal growth.

The schedule Jim had set for himself would exhaust and discourage anyone. Let's itemize it:

1. He set a health goal to be accomplished by getting up 90 minutes early. (Jim had previously done his workouts in the evenings, but he thought this was wasting too much time.)

2. He set a creative project goal, one with which he had no prior experience. But in the back of his mind, he'd always wanted to write a novel and resolving to make a dream a reality is to be respected in anyone.

3. He was going to enhance his professional standing by pursuing a graduate degree, the preparation for which had to be done over a period of time.

4. He wanted to change the place he lived and he set aside time to look for a new home.

5. He resolved to manage his money more wisely, and to that end, he signed up for an investment class.

6. Last, but not least, he took some action to find another significant relationship, because he had a goal to get married again.

Jim had attended a weekend motivational seminar and reinforced what he'd learned with tapes and books. So, overnight, he was transformed. Right? Wrong. Somewhere along the way, Jim came to believe that he must get started on everything at once. When it didn't work out perfectly—and the way he had set it up, it would have taken three people to do it—he thought that he just hadn't "gotten it," and was close to chucking the whole thing.

Jim hadn't even given himself credit for 1) taking the investment class, and 2) asking a woman he'd just met out for coffee. Those were actually steps along the way toward two goals. But, because Jim had no real system, no real plan, he couldn't see that he'd taken a couple of steps toward his quality life. In other words, he didn't have a quality mind approach in place. Jim's predicament is not unusual. As I've said, motivation is fine as far as it goes, but it doesn't work by itself. Jim is a clear example.

Our Friend Jim States His Vision

First, when we look at Jim's plan as outlined to Sally, can we clearly identify his vision? Does Sally know what he is about? Probably not. Let's backtrack, and pretend that Jim had decided to put a quality program into action. Where would he start? Most likely, Jim would spend some time thinking about his vision. Before he enumerated goals and rushed out to try to reach them, he might have set aside some time to write in a journal or sit quietly and think about the qualities he wanted in his life and the talents and skills he already has.

For example, let's look at the life Jim had before he decided that everything had to change in 24 hours. Jim is a statistician for an insurance company. He enjoys the work, but he knows that a computer science graduate degree would help him advance in his current company or a future one. His divorce occurred six months before we meet him and he lives in a small studio apartment. And, he admits he is lonely. Even though he works in a technical field, he has a creative bent, hence the urge to write. He has learned to paint and play a musical instrument, although he has lost some interest in those hobbies now. His divorce taught him that he should manage money in a more effective way—he and his wife had almost no assets to split. (They also had little to fight over—there is a silver lining in every cloud.) His doctor told him that at 40, he was in very good shape, but Jim forgot to give himself credit for sticking to an exercise program. Instead he tried to rearrange the schedule to fit it in among many new activities, a good idea in theory, but he was overtired because he was doing too much.

Let's see what kind of vision Jim could devise. When stated in its essence, Jim wanted a balance of creative variety in his life. Balance was what he craved—personally and professionally. He desired creative expression and technical excellence, but he had forgotten that his job did provide opportunities to be creative. In short, he separated the two areas, rather than realizing that he had already put a degree of balance in his life. He needed to build on it, but he should also give himself credit for what he had already achieved in this area.

So, a quality life for Jim could be summed up with the vision, "I want to express my creative talents in many areas—business, recreation, and in relationships." Whew! We can now let Jim relax a bit. He can take credit for the areas in which he has done this, he can examine the areas in which he doesn't experience the quality he wants, and now he can set some goals and take steps to form a plan to reach them. All he needs is a plan using the quality mind–quality life approach.

From Vision to Quality

In order to form goals and make plans, Jim will make use of all the resources in his inventory, (remember? ... RI), he will use all the skills we are discussing in this book, and he will identify which skills need enhancing first. Let's listen in as Jim analyzes what he wants, how he intends to get those things, and how he sets priorities.

Jim says to himself: "Since I can't do it all at once, where can I start? Where do I want to apply the quality ideas first? When I look at my job, I can see that I basically like it. Do I want to go to graduate school first and make it a priority, enabling me to get a new job or try for a promotion when I'm done? And, how long will it take? If I manage my money better, will I be able to get a better apartment a year from now? What do I need to do if I decide that I want to write a novel? Is a new relationship important to me? Where does it fit in with to my other goals, including education? How and when can I best go about getting it? Jim goes on to analyze his situation: "Last year, a woman at the office got time off and tuition reimbursement in order to pursue some courses that would help her on the job. Maybe I should see if that program is still open. Do I need a degree or just some new courses? When I think about it, I only need to learn some higher level computer skills to advance. Maybe I should start by exploring this option. I'll delay a final decision on my goal until I gather some information.

"Now, I know that I don't want to paint or play the flute anymore. It just isn't satisfying, but what would be? Okay, writing a novel. I feel that urge and I have a plot outline in my head and a few notes. What would move me along toward finishing this project? I could take a class, study with a published novelist, or read books about writing fiction. I could set aside a few hours a week and see if I like it."

Jim went on to look at his living situation and the relationship he wanted. "I really do want more people in my life, and I'd like to be married again. I also want to manage my money better and get a new apartment. There is something very strong that is pulling me to these things. Meeting new women and taking an investment class are the things that excite me the most."

Notice how our friend Jim has begun to narrow down some choices, has broken his goals into manageable pieces, and has given himself a chance to succeed. Furthermore, as we follow Jim along his quality life path, we can see that he will use the skills that make up the next section of this book. Negotiation, communication, organization, and decision-making will play roles no matter what Jim tries to tackle first.

Jim could hold his vision and check all his goals against that desire, that purpose, to live in a balanced way, expressing both his technical and creative leanings to be a productive professional and have a satisfying personal life. In fact, learning how to manage his money might end up being the foundation upon which he can build much of what he wants to do.

Some people would suggest that Jim's goals be set out in a five year or one year plan—this makes sense, but it isn't necessarily something that Jim needs to do today. Remember, Jim is beginning to put quality thinking into action. He is exploring and thinking creatively about himself and his life.

Jim Already has the Skills

What would happen if Jim concluded that because his first marriage ended in divorce, he has *no* communication skills? Would he not end up feeling like a complete failure? What if he concluded that because he couldn't make up his mind about graduate school, he didn't know how to make a decision? This would be erroneous at best, because Jim's process involves using all the skills to the extent he already has them. At worst, it would reinforce Jim's belief that if he can't get it all together immediately, he is not as good as other people—those mythical folks who seem to accomplish everything they set out to do.

If Jim had started with a vision, resulting from self-examination, he would not have started his life changes in such a self-defeating way. That's why I urge you to take the information in this book in a step-by-step manner. Yes, I want you to be motivated, and yes, I believe that you must start—somewhere—once you have formed your vision. But more than anything else, I want you to see quality living as an evolving system that combines the best of the personal growth movement and the quality movement in business.

It is obvious when we look at Jim's vision and his early attempts at a plan, he is creating quality in his life. How do we know this? Well, we can look at the things he is choosing. For example, when the idea of going to graduate school seemed overwhelming at the present time, Jim took a closer look at what he wanted the education to do for him. Furthermore, he recognized the possibility that his company might pay for his courses—a money management enhancer to be sure. Jim will use his negotiating and communication skills when he explores the program with management at the company, and he will lay the groundwork for future advancement. At the very least, he will go through the process of trying to get the best deal for himself at this time.

Jim wants to express himself creatively and manage his money. So, he decided to take an adult education class, which as it turned out, had some very appealing women in it. His investment class also offered opportunities for making new friends of both sexes. In a very real sense, Jim is working toward more than one goal at a time. He is adding quality in almost every area of his life. And, it is all being done in a manageable way. He is setting himself up for success, not failure.

No one can say how all Jim's desires will turn out. It is possible that he will hate creative writing. So what? He would never learn that unless he tried it. Painting might begin to look good to him again. It is also possible that Jim's company isn't interested in his graduate school plans. If that's the case, Jim can reevaluate his goal. He will know how important it is to him if he is faced with an obstacle. Clearly, we aren't going to make a value judgement here. You and I don't know if Jim should take classes or not. If we knew Jim, we might think he should be selling real estate or teaching school. That's not for us to decide.

A Quality Life—One Step At a Time

If I were working with Jim, I would urge him to put the process he's going through in writing, perhaps in the form of a weekly journal. I would also urge him to note each skill he uses as he thinks out and pursues his goals. I would tell him to look at his vision and make a clear statement about each action he takes as it relates to his vision. On the face of it, Jim's early decisions all serve his desire for creative balance in his life.

Finally, I would advise Jim to relate each step to his quality life goal. Is he giving and demanding quality every step of the way? It is possible that the creative writing teacher is not doing his or her job well? What will Jim do about that? Perhaps the investment class is taught by a sharp, informed person from whom Jim learns valuable skills. Will Jim drop the teacher a complimentary note when the class is over? What if a woman Jim meets is late for their dates or cancels frequently? Will Jim slink away or will he call the woman on her behavior and make it clear that it isn't acceptable? Is Jim making an effort to be on time himself and treat the women he dates with respect? How can he improve the quality he gives to those around him?

The first Jim story illustrates how motivation alone can be self-defeating if not combined with a quality management system. When Jim started out, he was filled with enthusiasm, dozens of dreams and goals, an "I can do it," attitude. But, in the end, it was an empty plan, because it was basically no plan at all. He wasn't better off than when he started; he was actually worse off because he ended his flush of motivation by giving up. Like all of us, Jim is only human; he needed time, patience, and gentle persistence. A quality approach provides the opportunity to create this climate in which real change can take place. He had the opportunity to use his Resource Inventory to help him every step of the way, and when he recognized a skill that needed improvement, he could work on it little by little.

So, Where Do You Begin?

Before you read further, why don't you begin to itemize those areas in your life you would like to enhance. Take as much time as you need—perhaps writing down your thoughts in a notebook as they come to you. Which area seems the most compelling? Perhaps, unlike Jim, you have a satisfying relationship, but your professional life is not so good. You might start there, and concentrate on your work life almost exclusively.

As you read through the next chapters, you may gain insight into the reasons you aren't happy with your work. Maybe you aren't negotiating well with your superiors, or you may have made some decisions that haven't worked out the way you thought. You may find that your choice was made in desperation—you had to have a job—and now you have more stability in your life and don't need that particular position anymore. But, you aren't giving yourself quality, because you haven't believed in the power to manage this area of life. However, you can now take charge and systematically put changes into effect.

Because so many of us have been affected by the "all or nothing" attitude, we may think that we can't be happy unless everything is right. But, when we have this mind-set, we have forgotten that life—and achievement and happiness—is a journey, not a destination. Jim, like many other people, learned that the power comes from exploring his options, making small changes, and learning along the way. Sure, Jim might have a set-back or two. But, because he now recognizes that he is on a journey, not an overnight self-improvement plan, he can relax and enjoy the ride.

I invite you to continue the work of putting your quality-oriented thinking in place.

Have you written down your vision? Do you know what you are about? Have you explored the areas in which you would like to implement the quality mind ideas first?

I have literally heard every imaginable area mentioned. Just last week, I talked to dozens of people who had heard me talk about achieving a quality life. When we discussed the life areas they thought they would apply the information to first, the diversity was astounding. Here's a sample:

- Bob wanted to improve communication with his five year old son. That was his overriding desire, taking precedence over his career goals.

- Diana wanted to improve communication with her co-workers, knowing that she had developed a reputation for being snobbish and hard to get along with. She also resolved to search for an answer to a persistent health problem—she was not giving herself quality treatment and that was most likely making communication more difficult.

- Larry wanted to find a life partner, and he needed to work on his tendency to isolate himself in his apartment. He couldn't get quality because he wasn't giving any. The first step Larry took was to volunteer for an organization he believed in. This was his way to meet new people in a structured setting.

- Anne asked for a raise, long overdue, and resolved to balance her check-book and prepare a budget. Money issues had so much "charge" on them that these were priorities. She couldn't think about anything else until she got this part of her life in order.

- Emily resolved to look for a new job—today. Her current position was taking every ounce of her energy and she was deeply unhappy every morning as she drove to her office.

- Arnie decided to buy a cabin on a lake and get away on the weekends with his family. He wanted to spend more time with his wife and children and have a chance to relax and read more. He liked his job, had plenty of money, but he didn't enjoy life as much as he wanted to.

- Mike made plans to finish high school, something he'd thought about for years. As a young person, he'd made some decisions that seemed okay at the time, but ultimately, he knew his life was going nowhere. At age 30, he was barely supporting himself with a minimum wage job and he still lived at home with his mother. He wanted to make *big* changes, but first things first. A high school diploma was a prerequisite to everything.

I could give dozens more examples of the ways in which people started putting quality ideas in place. In each of the above cases, there was some particular thing that the people needed to do in order to grasp the idea of adding quality—both delivering it to others and receiving it for themselves. And, each person was using specific skills to start the process of change.

Let's begin now to take a look at the basic skills we need to do just about everything in life. Remember, you aren't in the dark about these skills. You already have used them—you will be learning more, not starting from scratch. Ultimately, you will be calling upon these skills in every facet of your life, using quality mind–quality life concepts and watching your life prosper.

You are now ready to begin using these concepts with the set of fundamental skills you need to reach any goal. Communication, negotiation, and decision-making are a few of these essential abilities. The next chapter explores our ability and need to communicate effectively and artfully with those we care about. This in turn helps us manage conflict in our relationships and work to ensure we are understood as we intended. Remember that communication involves listening as well as talking and observing with our eyes as well as both listening and talking.

My colleague, author Eric Oliver, suggests that we liken communication to visiting a foreign country and you don't speak the language. In general, native speakers respond more favorably to you if you make some effort to communicate in their language. The amused or hostile reactions usually come when you think you'll communicate by speaking English ever more loudly and slowly. So, on a day-to-day basis, your effort to speak another's language is much like mirroring behaviors. You are establishing rapport by increasing comfort and empathy.

Put It Together

When we realize that there are many levels of communication, we become more sensitive to the needs of others and more in tune with them, not less sensitive. Developing communication skills will enhance quality thinking because we can open ourselves to the richness of mutually satisfying and beneficial relationships. Take this basic information and build on it. Observe and learn and improve the abilities you already have. It's a safe place from which to start—and succeed.

Your new understanding of communication will prove particularly beneficial when you enter into a negotiation. You may shrink from the very thought of negotiating, but trust me, this skill is not used only by politicians and lawyers. We all negotiate regularly, whether we are conscious of it or not. You already negotiate about something almost every day of your life. But now, you'll understand the process and gain confidence in your ability to bring new quality into your life.

CHAPTER V

Communication and Quality:
Listening, Watching, Talking

IT'S AN ALL TOO FAMILIAR SCENE: Mark is depressed because he believes he's a lousy communicator—he just can't seem to get the words right. In his mind, communication means the ability to tell others what he's thinking and feeling—and he thinks he does this poorly at best. Yet, Mark has a wide circle of friends, is close to his family, and does well in his computer consulting business. Still, he suffers from a sense that his life is not as pleasant or successful as it could be if he were able to communicate with others with greater ease.

I know Mark, however, and while he may not be the most articulate person, he is known among his friends as a terrific listener. In fact, I'd say that much of his success as a consultant stems from the fact that he knows how to listen to the problems his clients describe, take in and analyze the information, and then proceed to set up a terrific automated office that meets his clients' needs. To me, Mark has mastered one important component of communication, and that's the ability to listen.

You, like Mark and many other people, may be reading this chapter with a preconceived notion that you don't communicate well. Or, you may have breathed a bored sigh when you saw the chapter title and said, "Oh dear, someone else is going to tell me how important communication is—ho hum, as if I didn't know." Some people believe that communication is simply a matter of saying the right words at the right time in order to achieve a desired result. If they can't form the words, then they don't achieve the result. Therefore, they believe they can simply learn a mechanical formula and *voila!,* they'll be terrific at communication. But, as logical thinking would tell us, there is much more to human communication than a simple formula.

You Know More Than You Know

In this area, as in all the other skills we've been talking about, you are already an accomplished communicator. Think about this. If you have a job, you have communicated enough about your particular skills to an employer that he or she hired you. If you have a bank account, you have communicated with someone in order to set it up. You weren't turned away because you didn't say the right words well enough. If you have ever complained to the manager of a restaurant about the lousy service, you were involved in an interaction in which you had to both listen and talk. You may also have been conscious of watching, that is, watching for nonverbal cues that are included in so many of our human interactions. While much of the nonverbal communication that occurs between people is unconscious, we can learn to make ourselves aware of this important element of communication.

Think back to a situation in which you believed you communicated with another person and achieved a desired outcome. Perhaps it was during an important business negotiation or when you and your life partner made a significant compromise in an area that you disagreed about. Maybe communication with your parents or children had broken down, and you found a way to get beyond the impasse.

If you can, try to remember how you felt during these important minutes or hours. Did your body feel heavy or light? Did your voice sound even and clear? Were you filled with exhilaration or a sense of peace?

When we leave an encounter feeling buoyant and at peace with ourselves and others, we can usually say that the communication was a success. You have no doubt experienced this in your life, but you may not have given yourself credit for your achievement.

When we don't note the successes in our lives, we lose the opportunity to learn from them. That's right, we miss a chance to analyze what worked and then repeat the process in other situations. For example, when you and your business partner have a major disagreement the day after a successful negotiation, you are back to the place where you don't believe you can communicate effectively. You could say, "Hey, what worked yesterday? Let's try that and see if we can repeat our success."

Take a minute, grab a piece of paper, and without thinking too much, list the people with whom you believe you communicate well—at least most of the time. Mother, sister, father, brother, life partner or lover, business partner, best friend? How about the person who sells you a newspaper every morning, your doctor, dentist, lawyer, favorite teacher, boss, next door neighbor, your cousin Mary, or your uncle Jack? Your list may very well go on and on.

Now, turn the page over and list the people with whom you would like better communication—don't worry if some of the same people turn up on your list. It's likely that you and your partner or lover communicate well at least some of the time or you wouldn't be together at all. But, you may experience times when your communication breaks down and you want improvements. On the other hand, you may not interact with your sister in a mutually satisfactory way for even five minutes. You and your childhood friend may not understand each other very well and it's bothered you all along. Later, you will learn a few tips that will immediately improve communication with people on both lists.

Before we continue, however, be assured that from the minute you were born, you were (and are) communicating. If you hadn't done it well at least some of the time, it isn't likely you'd be reading this book right now. Furthermore, you've established relationships with people who have responded to you and have shown a willingness to engage in an ongoing two-way communication. You already have communication skills in your Resource Inventory—now you want to sharpen those skills, learn more about the art and science of communication, and then use what you learn to create your quality life.

We're All in this Together

When you considered your Resource Inventory, you learned that the people in your life are important entries on the list. No matter what you want to achieve in life, you need other people. Some have considered this a sign of weakness and will build walls around themselves and declare: "I don't need anyone—I'm going it alone." This is an illusion at best, and a tragic denial of our shared humanity at worst. It's also a lonely way to live.

The essence of communication involves the recognition that it involves two or more people, and includes everything that defines them as unique individuals. When I talk to Mary, an individual, I'm communicating with a person who is a particular age, sex, race, and who is from a particular psychosocial background. She has a certain degree of intelligence, a unique storehouse of information, and she has formed certain attitudes and beliefs that come together to define her.

I may not talk to Mary in precisely the same way I talk to Mark, because each has unique attributes. Mary is outgoing and vivacious; Mark is quiet and appears shy. But my two acquaintances share a common humanity and they are important to me for different reasons. The way I interact with Mary is neither better nor worse than the way I approach Mark—it's just different.

When you begin to absorb and use the ideas in this chapter, think about the benefits that will be afforded all the people in your life. You may find that you serve as a catalyst to improve relationships all around you. Relationships always change when one person changes. In this case, you are improving your communication skills, and the tone and nature of your interactions are bound to change—and I can almost guarantee they will change for the better.

Communication as Shared Meaning

Mark doesn't believe he's a proficient communicator because he thinks that the concept refers to his ability to talk. He has formed the impression that words are the most important element in communication. However, the words we choose can be understood in many ways. Sure, it's easier to interact when we experience shared meaning. When I talk with another lawyer, we use certain words and phrases; to a non-lawyer our conversation sometimes could sound like a form of verbal shorthand.

However, shared meaning goes far beyond a simple shared language. Ultimately, shared meaning can be defined as people who bring all their individual characteristics and experiences to an interaction and, consciously or unconsciously, attempt to establish a context in which to communicate. That sounds fancier than it needs to, but it's still true.

Much miscommunication results when we don't understand or care to acknowledge the importance of shared meaning. I invite a friend to join me for dinner at a steak house. My friend, unbeknownst to me, is a vegetarian. My friend looks insulted and snaps a refusal of my invitation at me. I walk away wondering what got into him. I do know that we didn't have shared meaning in our interaction, but I don't know the particulars.

When a baby cries, parents try to figure out what he or she is communicating. They offer food and the baby lets out more angry cries. So far, there's no shared meaning. They change the baby's diaper and the crying turns into cooing. Now we have shared meaning. You see, communication does not require the words to match the metaphorical music. You just need to find the beat and match the tune and the words will find their way.

When we consider how easy it is to miscommunicate when we share many cultural attributes, it's no wonder that we have so much trouble interacting when shared meaning is marginal or difficult to achieve. However, the lack of an obvious shared context doesn't mean that we can't have effective interactions. Perhaps we must work harder to achieve an "atmosphere" of shared meaning.

Being Precise

There are a few simple tips that can help improve communication immediately, and I do mean immediately. In addition, practicing these tips can help you in situations in which communication is bound to be more complex.

To begin, consider the following statements:

"Uh, would you like to go out sometime?"

"Don't you think you overcooked the vegetables?"

"Your work will have to improve—soon."

"I need some money for my business."

"You're always late."

"You never say anything nice."

"Every man lets me down."

"All women play games."

"You're just like all the others."

"Kids just don't care about anything these days."

"They should fix the health care system."

"What a lousy idea."

"His speeches infuriate me."

"She irritates me no end."

When we look at each statement, we would probably agree that none is a particularly good example of positive communication. But in addition, these statements aren't effective either—not even in their negative intent. Neither the listener nor the speaker are any better off than when they started.

Neither knows what the objective is; neither knows what a positive outcome would be; and, neither has any reason to continue a conversation. In some cases, some specific questions could lead to clarification, but the statements don't invite further interaction. Yet, not one of these statements is original or even uncommon. Daily conversation is littered with statements just like those above. No wonder we feel dazed sometimes.

If you were the person to whom the first statement was directed, what would you think, much less say? Many a man or woman has felt rejected after asking for a date in such a vague way. What does "go out" mean? What does "sometime" mean? When two old friends meet on the street, they might agree to "get together sometime." When they're both that vague, you can bet there's ambivalence about ever meeting again. Chances are no future meeting will take place, at least until their next embarrassed chance encounter.

Well, the same goes for the social invitation that is nonspecific and vague. Consider the statement: "Would you like to go to the play at the Strand theater on Friday night?" This is a lot different from the vague request in the first statement. The receiver hears a straightforward invitation that calls for a specific answer. The person could say, "Yes, I'd like that," or "I'm sorry, I've made plans for Friday—how about Saturday instead?", or "I'm busy then, but thanks for asking." Each statement delivers a clear message, and each person is clear about what is being said.

The second statement is one I actually overheard in a restaurant. The patron was not satisfied with the food and wanted it sent back. But the statement is calculated to confuse the issue and an argument ensued. How much more effective it would have been if the man had simply said, "The dinner you brought isn't acceptable. The vegetables are overcooked and the steak is far too rare. Please take it back." The waiter has a clear message to communicate to the kitchen staff, but doesn't feel belittled or insulted. In most situations, the kitchen will correct the mistake and everyone wins.

In both of our examples, the speaker did not communicate a clear objective when the statement was made. Establishing our purpose—our objective—is one of the most important tips we can put into action immediately. Try it and see for yourself that it works.

If I approach a person and say, "I need money for my business," I am offering vague information. What do I need the money for—equipment, marketing, personnel, advertising? How much money do I need? Am I making a cloaked request or am I just stating a fact? Unfortunately, many people end up making these statements with the hope that the listener will say, "Okay, how much do you want?" Now we all know this kind of response is rare.

What would happen if I approach a friend and say, "I need $5,000 for office equipment and some training that will help me use it effectively. I'd like to borrow the money and will pay interest on the loan. If you're interested, this is how I would pay it back." And the explanation follows.

My friend could say, "That sounds like a wise investment. But we'll have to talk about the payment schedule before we work up the final contract." A negotiation is under way. Or, she could say, "I'm committed to some other projects right now, but I have an uncle who would like to earn higher interest on his money. Let's talk to him." Or, perhaps she's not interested at all. Her response might be, "I'm not looking at personal loans as a way to invest. I'm not interested in hearing more about this." If she is a good friend, she might add, "Is there some other way I could help you?"

In actuality, a friend of mine was approached in this way and ended up helping a friend borrow the money from her bank. In another situation, money for a business venture did indeed come from the proverbial "rich uncle." In the latter case, there was a perceived value in hearing the person out. The uncle could make some money too, and it was a win-win situation all around.

During the next few days, listen to your own manner of communicating.

Do you have an objective when you make a request? Are you clear about what you want? Do you use words that convey your need?

Listen for vague statements, ones that sound either sarcastic or belittling or offer no way to clearly respond to the need you have.

Consider the statements that include the universals—you *never,* you *always, all* women, *every* man, and so on. There are also the implied universals. "Kids nowadays" do such and such, for example, implies that all young people are the same. We hear these universals so much that we may be unconsciously using them ourselves.

If a person cares about you or about the subject matter, he or she might consider asking you specific questions, or the listener could make sympathetic comments, such as, "I'm sorry that man dumped you," or, "It's too bad you had such a bad experience with that woman." Much of the time, however, people will nod their heads and continue on with their own thoughts and preoccupations. Some people will agree wholeheartedly and tell you a horror story of their own. This might be a form of commiseration—as in "misery loves company," but it won't do much to help us grow—and it certainly doesn't lead to a quality mind. Participating as a listener/commiserator won't add quality to our life either. When you want to add quality to your life, you will find that speaking in the vague language of universals detracts from your efforts.

In a similar way, examine the statements that dismiss ideas or plans and shut communication down. "What a lousy idea," or, "That will never work," are statements that leave no place to go with the conversation. The person whose plan or idea it was in the first place will probably simply shut up and go away.

In her book, *Women Who Run With the Wolves,* author Clarissa Pinkola Estes advises readers to stay away from *anyone* who tramples on an idea. If they are people who are close to you in other ways, you may still want to love them, but you don't have to let them slaughter your ideas. This is a crucial concept in any quality life program. Remember that most of us have been socialized to be polite in most situations and we may not exercise our freedom to tell this negative person that we don't appreciate these comments.

Many of us also respond more directly, and sometimes more hurtfully, to people we know well than we do when talking to strangers. For example, your brother would probably never tell a stranger that his or her idea is stupid, but he might not hesitate to say that to you. Dr. Estes' point here is that this dismissal and the refusal to even talk about an idea kills creativity and undermines a sense of personal power and autonomy. When you think about the people in your Resource Inventory, pay close attention to the way they respond to you—and you to them. If thoughtless negativity and quick dismissal of your ideas are elements of your communication, consider this the way you would consider poison—dangerous to your health. Don't forget that poison has no part in your quality life program.

An appropriate response from a loving, caring person might be, "Tell me more, I don't understand, and I want to learn more about your idea." Nurturing people will always ask questions and attempt to find something in an idea that they can relate to. Remember: listen to the way you respond to people, too. This isn't a one-way street. You're offering quality as well as demanding it.

Depending on the circumstances of having your idea summarily dismissed, you might probe further about what exactly is "lousy" about it. "Why don't you think it will work?" you ask. Or, "What is bad about my plan? Can you be more specific?" In some situations, this does open a line of communication, as the saying goes. But in other situations, the person might simply shrug off the question and not have anything specific to offer. Here, too, is a message.

Sheer logic tells us that if an idea appears to be poor, bad, foolish, or whatever, there must be some reason for that evaluation. You are not obligated to hang around and wait for a person to come up with more vague notions—"It just isn't realistic." or, "I don't know, it just won't work."

Vague statements can lead to many kinds of reactions. Consider the statement, "Your work will have to improve—soon." Darrell, a man in one of my seminars was told this by his supervisor and he concluded that he was being put on notice. He had no idea what part of his work wasn't satisfactory and he immediately began to look for another job. A month later he gave two weeks notice on his job and his supervisor was shocked! Why would Darrell leave a company where he was doing so well? Darrell was confused and never did learn what the supervisor's complaint was. He's happy in his new job, but he wonders just how communication with his supervisor became so confused. (Darrell and millions of other people!)

When we are on the receiving end of vague statements, we can start—today—to ask questions. Like journalists, we can begin with who, what, when, where, why. Who should fix the health care system? What exactly is it that you don't like about my plan (or my clothes or car or values)? When would you like to get together? When will the money be paid back? When will the new shipment of widgets be in? Where would you like to have dinner? Where (and who) are all these people who are holding you back and keeping you from reaching these goals? Why are you dissatisfied with my work? Why were you unable to be here on time? Why don't you approve of my business plan?

In this section, you have two basic suggestions to follow. One, watch your own use of vague statements and the universal, all encompassing words and phrases. Two, begin to improve communication with others by asking questions that will reveal the thoughts behind the vague responses you get.

I've spoken with many people who have tried these two suggestions for just a few days and were amazed at the results. For example, Helen was able to break away from some negative people, who for years had laughed off her ideas to complete a graduate degree. Two or three "what and why" questions made it clear to her that there was no thought-out reason for this negativity. And she'd been taking it personally for years! This small incident changed the way she viewed communication. Helen also learned that she was far too dependent on the opinion of others, and she began to reexamine her desire to go back to school.

In another case, Al borrowed money for a business venture after he had clearly outlined his objectives. For several months, he had been approaching some family members with only a statement of his need for money. He hadn't told them what it was for or how they would benefit from helping him. Once Al was able to articulate his plan, the vague need was replaced by a clear goal.

And, a word about the universal statements. Anyone with the intelligence to read this book knows that *all* men, women, Catholics, Jews, Muslims, African Americans, Italians, Hispanics, Russians, Germans, doctors, lawyers, teachers, young people, and so on, don't think or act alike. The fact that sweeping statements are still made reflects a form of mental sloppiness. We know better, and we communicate far more effectively when our language reflects it.

In his book, *The Human Factor at Work,* human development and communication specialist, Eric Oliver, points out the way we sometimes talk to ourselves—our thinking habits. For example, we might say, "I really want to go out with that woman, it's the *only* thing that will satisfy me. I'll be *miserable* until I see her again." Oliver calls this an example of a "scarcity" thinking habit. When we decide that one particular thing is the only thing that will satisfy us, and that we will be miserable without this one thing, we have formed the habit of thinking in impoverished—scarcity—terms.

What if we were to think, "I will make an arrangement to see that person again. I know I will enjoy myself—but I can't predict what will happen during our evening. If I can't see her, then this one area of life won't be as pleasant as I'd like, but I'll try to meet someone else that attracts me as much as she does." Oliver calls this "possibility" thinking.

If you find yourself using terms like "impossible," or "rare," or you say that the chances of something happening are "less than zero," then you have probably formed the habit of scarcity thinking. But, if you use such words and phrases as "challenging," or "risky but worth it," you may have developed "possibility thinking." Now possibility thinking can be negative as well as positive. For example, colorful possibility thinkers use phrases like, "we're on a slippery slope of danger."

Watch that language too, even in your own mind and heart. You may find that the supposedly innocent statements you make, using universal words or vague statements, for example, have served to limit your expectations and desires. We certainly know that these limiting words and phrases reflect our inner beliefs in deprivation and scarcity.

Over the next month or so, note the situations in which communication was halted, stopped in its own tracks, by the use of negative or vague statements or by the vague, but all encompassing "universals," including those words and phrases that imply scarcity and lack of possibilities. The second step is to note those situations in which you chose to break the pattern of the interaction and tried something new.

What were the outcomes? How did you feel when the conversation was over? What did you learn that can help you develop a quality mind—and a quality life?

The Importance of Establishing Rapport

If we replace universal statements and vague requests with concrete words and specific ideas, then we have taken a big step toward establishing rapport with other people. For the sake of simplicity, let's define rapport as a bond, a sense of comfort, or an atmosphere of ease between two or more people. When we have rapport, communication generally proceeds smoothly. We may not agree with the person on every point or we may have a different idea about the outcome of a problem we must solve, but our rapport makes a meaningful discussion possible.

There are people with whom we say we have "instant rapport." We say we are on the same wave length, we find we can almost finish one another's sentences, or we seem to know what the other person is thinking. We appear to be of one mind, and at times, this kind of relationship can seem almost magical. We don't know why it happens, but we enjoy it and feel energized when we encounter these people.

What if we could create this rapport with more of the people we interact with? What if we found a way to look for the common ground before we start a negotiation, or before we hire a person to work for us, or before we choose an accountant, lawyer, doctor, or some other professional?

Perhaps we could attempt to establish a degree of this kind of rapport with every person we meet, from our troublesome parent to the clerk in the store. It's possible if we work at it—and just think about what it would do to bring quality into our lives.

If we surround ourselves with people who are going after their dreams and working toward their goals, we will find ourselves able to establish close bonds and to be in a similar emotional and mental place. A scenario of rapport includes the natural exchange of ideas and enthusiasm for the goals that others are trying to reach. The question, "How can I help you?", might replace the closed thought of, "What's in this for me?"

So, How Do We Establish Rapport?

We find common ground with some people easily and effortlessly, barely giving it a thought. As we move through life we'll periodically encounter people with whom rapport is almost instant. However, in other situations we must create rapport. And it starts with us and our attitude. If we don't see an obvious area of common ground, then perhaps we'll have to find one.

One way you can do this is by being a good listener. You can ask questions and wait for answers before you inject your own opinion. Like Mark, who asks question after question about his clients' needs

QUALITY MIND, QUALITY LIFE

and then works hard to meet them, you can find the areas in which you can agree or have a mutual goal.

People have told me that this process of seeking common ground is an effective way to *reestablish* rapport with their teenagers. One father told me that the only common ground he and his daughter could find was concern for her safety—late hours, what would the neighbors think, the fact that alcohol is illegal for minors, her falling grades, and so on, did not constitute common ground. But, this adolescent agreed that she didn't want to die. At last, something they could agree on. It doesn't sound like much, but it reopened a way to communicate that had been closed for years. She believed her father loved her and wanted her to be safe, and that fact enabled them to talk about consequences of her behavior.

Common ground is also a requirement before any negotiation can begin. Are we both talking about a sale of property and do we both want the sale to reach completion? We might find that the person is ambivalent about selling or ambivalent about buying. What if we learned this early in the negotiation process? We could find ourselves at decision points that we might not have thought of before. Let's say that the ambivalence was not going to be overcome. Rather than attempting to buy a property that isn't actually for sale, we could withdraw and move on. Or, we could find that the ambivalence actually has to do with price or timing. Perhaps there are steps to take that could correct these problems and allow us to continue.

Many wise people have commented that they learned a lot more by asking questions than by continuing to defend their own position. Finding common ground often requires us to focus less on ourselves and more on the other person. It may also demand that we become active observers of body language.

In the field called Neurolinguistic Programming (NLP), Richard Bandler, John Grinder and the many who followed them describe a process called "mirroring," which is a way to establish common ground and therefore, rapport, through matching another person's interest, opinion, or idea. However, since much of communication is nonverbal, we can mirror or match the person's body language. For instance, we can adjust our tone of voice or our posture to match that of the person we are talking with. This is often an unconscious process, in that the other person becomes more comfortable with you because you seem to be more like him or her.

Quality communication is not about manipulation, however, it is about rapport and finding common ground. Many people have taken these techniques and viewed them as a way to get control or power in a situation—power over another person. We're talking about ways to understand other people and establish rapport, but we aren't suggesting that these techniques be used to gain control over others. At its best, communication is about creating quality for ourselves and by association, for others.

The field of NLP points out that people express their ideas in ways that represent a particular way of viewing the world. Some people are visual. They say such things as: "I just can't picture that happening," or, "I don't see what you mean." Others are auditory and may say, "I don't hear that the way you do" or "Is this loud and clear?" Other people express themselves in a manner that reflects a more kinesthetic relationship with the world. These people talk about ideas "touching" them, or something "feels" right—"solid," "firm," or "hot," or "cold." And idea that leave one person cold might make another person warm up. A person who is visual might need a "clear picture," and the same idea might need to "sound right" to the auditory person.

As another exercise, listen carefully to the way people you interact with use language. Can you identify a dominate style in the way they express their attitudes and opinions? If you consciously begin

QUALITY MIND, QUALITY LIFE

to use words that match their own, do you sense a shift in the way your communication is going? Again, this is not for the purpose of manipulating; this is a way to understand and establish common ground and rapport.

We can observe body language as well.

Is the person you're communicating with saying one thing, but doing another? For example, is the person telling you that your idea sounds great, but he or she is backing away from you—even subtly bending slightly backwards? Or, is the person leaning toward you and perhaps matching your posture? How do you react to these two different forms of body language?

Body language is a complex subject, but when you begin observing, you'll find yourself able to form impressions quickly and more easily than you might imagine. You already do this—you simply may not be conscious of the way this has affected communication with others. In the previously mentioned book, Eric Oliver discusses the importance of nonverbal cues. He indicates, among other points, that we often send messages with our head nods and movements because our internal processing precedes the words we verbalize. In addition, he points out that we often indicate the expected answers to the questions we ask by nodding our head in the direction of the expected response. These natural movements can bias the response we get from the person with whom we are speaking since people will unconsciously perceive the expected nonverbal message that accompanies the words we use.

If you have any doubt about the importance of nonverbal communication, wander around in a crowd by yourself, which gives you an opportunity to observe. Oliver suggests that we can almost always tell who is together in a long line at a theater, for example, even when the people aren't talking. Observe this for yourself—make conscious what has been below the conscious level until now. Watch how couples mimic one another's gestures—even the angry ones. See how parents match the facial expressions of their children. You may see that people lean toward and away from one another at the exact same moments in shared conversations.

You may also see mixed messages being sent. For example, you may see one person earnestly lean forward, while another person simultaneously leans backward and away. You may see someone looking over another person's head into the crowd, as if listening is merely a chore and not to be taken seriously.

As you observe others, begin observing yourself. You may find that you send mixed messages, too. One way we improve communication with others is by realizing that it all comes back to us. Remember, a quality life is your responsibility. You can't control how others respond to you, but you can control how you choose to communicate and the way in which you respond to others. Remember that communication involves listening as well as talking, and observing with our eyes as well as both listening and talking.

Eric Oliver suggests that we liken communication to visiting a foreign country where you don't speak the language. In general, native speakers respond more favorably to you if you make some effort to communicate in their language. The amused or hostile reactions usually come when you think you'll communicate by speaking English ever more loudly and slowly. So, on a day-to-day basis, your effort to speak another's language is much like mirroring behaviors. You are establishing rapport by increasing comfort and empathy.

Put it Together

When we realize that there are many levels of communication, we become more sensitive to the needs of others and more in tune with them, not less sensitive. Developing communication skills will enhance our lives because we can open ourselves to the richness of mutually satisfying and beneficial relationships. Take this basic information and build on it. Observe and learn and improve the abilities you already have. It's a safe place from which to start—and succeed.

One valuable arena to measure success is in our negotiations with others, offering us opportunities to experience the give and take of human interaction.

CHAPTER VI

Negotiating Brings Quality

NOT LONG AGO, I ASKED A GROUP OF PEOPLE to tell me what they thought of when they heard the word "negotiation." I wanted them to tell me the first thing that came to mind. The range of responses was fascinating. Most people answered by naming specific situations, rather than indicating knowledge of the concept or a definition of a process or an action. "Settling on the price of something—like a house," one man said. "Ending a war," a woman offered, and added, "when both sides are in bad shape and there's no other choice."

Someone else pointed out that negotiation is something that should take place before a war starts, but seldom does. But one young person simply said, "Negotiation means winning when I argue with my parents about the time I have to be home on weekend nights." To this young man, negotiation is all about getting something—being a winner in relation to another person.

There were a couple of responses that indicated that negotiation involved give and take—a win some, lose some description of the outcome. Other people, however, had a strong sense that in almost any negotiation, there was a winner and a loser, and losing would always be a diminishing experience. Only one person believed that he was an accomplished negotiator, and that impression was formed based on how often he succeeds when he dickers over the price of antiques that he buys for his home.

The responses were not out of the ordinary. I hear them frequently when I give my talks to groups both large and small. Most people, unless it is a defining part of their profession, believe that negotiation is something other people need to engage in. Furthermore, most people believe that the ability to negotiate is an attribute, something that people are born capable of doing. If you weren't born with this talent, then poor you, all you can do is struggle along. For example, the woman who saw negotiation as something world leaders do, or should do, thought that the people sent to do the job most likely had a natural tendency to be effective at the task.

The idea that the ability to negotiate is a learned skill is simply not part of most people's consciousness. But, I assure you, the ability to negotiate is not innate; it is learned through formal education and it is perfected through practice and experience. Why is this important in a quality life? Because personal management relies on specific fundamental skills, used in almost all situations we encounter in our lives.

The previous chapter, and now this one, discusses a set of key communication-related skills that we need to succeed in achieving whatever vision and goals we establish for our life. You use negotiating skills from the moment you wake up in the morning until you go to bed at night.

Will you get up to go to work? Where will you eat lunch? Can you get a raise at work? Will you see a movie this evening? And on and on. We negotiate the answers to these and many questions all day long, based on a particular set of facts that accompany each question. We may negotiate a situation that results in our not getting up for work—perhaps we agreed to work late three nights in order to have three mornings off. We may see a movie, a play, or go to the bowling alley, depending on the outcome of negotiations with our friend or partner.

The process is so much a part of our lives that we're often unaware that we're doing it. This chapter will take what you do naturally, bring it into your consciousness, and suggest how to do it most effectively.

Without even knowing you or knowing anything about you, I'm already convinced that you have extensive experience with negotiation. From the time you were a small child, you learned to make a case for a position you held or a desire you wanted to have fulfilled. As you grew older, you learned there were some situations in which negotiation was not an option, nor was your desire to engage in some give and take appreciated by your parents or teachers. You may have concluded that negotiation involves power, and you also may have decided that you didn't have the power that enabled you to engage in negotiation.

Well, it's time to think again. You do have power—over your own life and your own immediate circumstances. You have the power to choose what you want and the power to attempt to get it. You also have the power to work with others to get the practical help, advice, and emotional support you need to advance toward your goals, guided by your vision. Therefore, you aren't learning the skill of negotiation from scratch, but your job now is to improve on the skill you already use.

Take a minute and write down all the situations in which you negotiated something over the past several days. Remember, these situations do not need to be monumental, nor must they have affected your life in a substantial way. When I asked Andrea, a friend of mine, to name some situations during the previous week that required negotiation, she came up with the following list:

- She had gone to her boss on behalf of a person who worked under her and negotiated a sudden change in vacation scheduling. It took about five minutes to work out a new plan.

- Her five-year-old wanted fast food for dinner. Andrea negotiated an order of french fries to go along with the more healthful dinner she fixed at home. The five-year-old felt like a winner.

- She negotiated an increase in pay for her day-care provider who had been with her for four years. The woman needed more money; my friend needed the continuity of care for her child. Both had strong, valid needs to consider. The negotiation took place over a period of four days. Each needed to think about the possibilities and implications of the proposals raised.

- She changed a lunch date with her sister who had some important family business to discuss. Her sister wanted the meeting immediately, but my friend negotiated for the lunch to take place on a day that she had the time to spend without feeling pressured by other appointments.

- When her dry cleaner ruined a blouse, Andrea pushed for a settlement that, while not completely compensating her for the loss, was better than the first offer, which was ridiculously low. She also changed dry cleaners. Quality is important to her and the mistake didn't bother her as much as the owner's hedging behavior and reluctance to take responsibility.

Andrea named three or four upcoming situations in which she needed to ask for a change in some circumstance in her life. She was well aware that she would use, to a greater or lesser degree, her negotiating skills. Perhaps Andrea was certain about this because she is a businesswoman and is aware of the process and uses it regularly with her clients.

Because we are all unique, we will each come up with a different list. Some people may spend much of their time negotiating with people at home or at school. Others will think about the skill as one that is work-connected in some way. Still others will think of it as almost entirely involved with "deals" of some kind—mainly buying and selling.

Right now, make your list and be as inclusive as possible. Don't make judgements about yourself or those with whom you were negotiating. Simply name the situations. When you're done, think of each situation and link it, even in a small way, to a quality life. Does the negotiation further your vision? Does it require the use of other resources in your life? Did these negotiations add quality to your life, or, perhaps reduce quality?

Are you finding the task difficult? Does the connection between your pursuit of quality and balance in your life and these situations seem illusive?

Perhaps this is an entirely new way of thinking for you. You may not have considered these kinds of events in your life as having any particular importance, or as involving negotiation. You are now coming to realize that every time you engage in the process of negotiating, you are exercising a fundamental skill.

In addition, you are affecting some circumstance in your life—for better or for worse with each negotiation result. If you decided not to go to work, perhaps it cost you wages. Or, if you went to a movie last night, perhaps you were tired at work the next day or missed an important telephone call that came while you were out. On the other hand, you may have been enriched by the experience, refreshed by taking time off, or drawn closer to the friend you were with. Anything is possible.

By now, I hope you are thinking about negotiation and the role it plays in your life. Whether you are conscious of it or not, your present circumstances are the result of numerous decisions, many of which were the result of negotiation with yourself and others. You decided what was important to keep or have or do, and you made trade-offs in order to achieve what you thought was best at the time.

Take an Attitude Check

Before you begin to consciously improve your negotiating skill, it's important to recognize and examine your beliefs and attitudes about the process. Do you, like many people, and my teenage acquaintance, believe that a negotiation is successful only when one person wins and the other one loses? Some people believe that a war isn't won until the opponent is completely destroyed. Others believe that they lose if every term isn't met exactly to their specifications. Do you believe that negotiating is about power and deception or about cooperation and honesty?

Perhaps you consider yourself a cooperative and honest person, and therefore, you anticipate losing in any negotiation because you are often up against someone who fails to share your concern with cooperative win-win results. If you view negotiation as essentially an adversarial process, you may be keeping yourself at a disadvantage.

Negotiation is a process in which everyone wants to do as well as they can for themselves. There is always a sense of competition present, but there is also a component of cooperation used by every negotiator if resolution is ever achieved. Negotiation is essentially a process of give and take. The satisfactory conclusion of a business deal, resolving potential or personal conflict, or preventing or stopping violence between two warring countries are, in truth, proof that human beings recognize their interdependence. We need and desire to live comfortably with each other and to respect others' points of view. At times, to be sure, it doesn't look as if this is the root reason that the process of negotiation developed, but it is. We negotiate because we don't live in this world alone and we would like to keep it that way. In fact, we consider this process so important that at times we hire other people to do it for us. This has advantages, but it has some disadvantages too. For one, many of us believe that only professionals are good at negotiation, and we discount that we, too, can develop this skill and use it to help us get what we need or want.

Negotiation is not only an inherently ethical process, it is one that serves the higher good of bringing people together. We bring our religious beliefs, our professional ethics, our personal set of standards, and our values to each negotiation. If we violate our own standards, our self-esteem suffers and we never feel positive about the outcome. And, of course, we need to be aware of the values and standards of those with whom we negotiate. This is as true of personal negotiations as it is of those that we think of as formal and related to our professional or work lives.

Negotiating Your Way to the Top

It should be obvious that we use negotiation in every part of our life, and while the applications are different, the same set of skills are used. For now, when you begin to imagine your life as you would like it to be, let us place focus on your work life and the role that the negotiation plays there. I've selected this setting because it most often involves negotiating with others who have a consistent presence in your life for a significant part of each day.

As constant as work is in our lives, we change jobs over the years and coworkers come and go as well. Therefore, this is an excellent and fluid environment to consider the flexibility we need each time we employ negotiating skills.

Using and improving your negotiating skills is an integral part of taking control of your career. Since we spend almost one third of our lives engaged in some form of work, it's an important area in which to start practicing. Start by thinking back over the work-related negotiating you have already done. For some people, this is obvious. Their day may be characterized by a series of negotiations—settling disputes, finalizing sales, keeping a classroom full of children occupied and happy, and so on.

Others might not be aware of the negotiating they actually do, or the opportunities that are available if they choose to take advantage of them. Take the issue of compensation and salary. I'm amazed at how many people take the salaries and increases that are offered to them, but never think that they can negotiate or renegotiate the terms under which they work. For example, Richard, a man in one of my workshops had assumed that everyone in his particular job category made about the same amount of money. He was amazed that other people— his peers—were all making higher salaries. He shouldn't have been so surprised since these other people had asked for raises, but he had not.

Richard is not the first person who simply didn't understand the tactics of the workplace. His parents had both worked in companies where salaries were negotiated by union representatives and the negotiating was done for them. They measured their increases in terms of wins and losses negotiated by their union. This was appropriate to his parents' situation, but it did not apply to Richard's current circumstance. Meanwhile, Richard struggled along, and took what was offered and didn't ask too many questions or make too many demands.

In order for Richard to change his life for the better, he had to take charge of his own earning power. This was a big step for him. When I spoke with him after the seminar, he expressed some hope mixed with apprehension. He wanted to take charge, but he wasn't sure where to start. Should he storm into the boss's office and make demands? Should he make the boss aware that he knew he was paid less than his peers? Should he express anger over being left out? Or, should he ask in a polite voice for some form of justice? What should he do if the boss refused to give him a raise?

Richard's imagination was working at full speed. It wasn't long before he pictured himself fired and out on the street. Is this an extreme case? I don't think so. Richard simply didn't know—yet— how to think out the dilemma and come to a position that would both satisfy him and be possible to get. The first thing Richard needed to do was to create a situation of choice for himself.

Too often, people accept whatever is given to them. This is clearly not a situation of choice, but rather is one similar to a robotic state— no choice, no options. In other situations, we are faced with an "either-or" situation. We can take what is offered, or not take it. This, too, is not a situation of choice, but rather it is a dilemma. The only way to create a situation of true choice is to have at least three options from which to choose. If you can take the offered terms, reject them, or make a counter-proposal, then a significant sense of freedom is created and pressure is considerably reduced. We all need to find choices in any negotiation setting; this means working to find or create at least three options.

Thinking Out a Position—What Do You Want?

One of the reasons so many of us don't get what we want is that we are like Richard, and we don't have a plan, or a formal position that we are after. While a salary negotiation is but one of the many kinds of career related negotiations, it serves as a good example of the steps involved in preparing for a negotiation because it is often the most nerve wracking experience we encounter in our employment.

Each negotiation requires us to think out the strategy, the execution, and the consequences. In practical terms for Richard, this meant looking at the way he should approach his boss, how much information he should reveal, and determining what is a realistic outcome. Other elements might be involved, such as the timing and setting of the negotiation. These are very important too. In a general sense, each negotiation means extensive preparation before undertaking the effort.

You can't avoid, nor should you short circuit, appropriate preparation prior to each negotiation. In fact, preparing for the interaction may be the single most important factor to success; without it, risks increase dramatically for concession and weakness. If this sounds complex, let's remember that some issues are more complicated than others.

Let's take Richard through the steps of preparation he must go through *before* he approaches his boss. First, Richard needs to assess what he already knows. For example, he learned the range of salaries made by his coworkers. He needs to analyze that information to make sure that their jobs are comparable. In other words, is he really being paid less for exactly the same work? He concludes that yes, they were all doing the same job, and all had the same title.

Richard also needs to examine how long each of his coworkers has been with the company relative to him. As it turned out, he had been there longer than his coworkers and had previously held two other positions in the company. He actually had the most years with the company, which added to his anxiety about negotiating a raise. If he suddenly changed his behavior, he reasoned, would that make his boss suspicious? Would they then fire him?

All this might sound odd to a seasoned negotiator or to a person with more confidence in their work skills. However, Richard and many people like him, operate out of fear much of the time. Should he ignore the fear and plunge in? Probably not. In my experience as an attorney, I've found that most people need to spend time with their fears—enough time to examine them carefully. Richard needs to face the fear and look at its source before proceeding.

Like many people in his age group—late 40s—he was raised by people who had lived through the Depression of the 1930s. He was raised to believe that just having a job made him a lucky man. (We've all noticed that this attitude is beginning to again seep back into public consciousness.) While his parents had relied on their unions to protect them from losing their jobs, these attitudes and circumstance did not, however, apply to Richard. He had to do something else. But it was important for him to look at his attitude and the deep-seated fear that he could be fired for making a single demand.

Because of his background, Richard would have been far more comfortable being part of a group for which hired negotiators handled salary matters. But, if he is going to get what he wants, he'll have to overcome this discomfort and fear of change. No one else can do this for him. Preparation will be the key to erasing the fear.

Let's assume that Richard properly prepared and gathered the information he needed. For some people, this might be a five minute process, but for others, and for Richard, this examination and information gathering took a few weeks. Is this a waste of time? Hardly. These weeks were probably among the most important in his life. No, this is not hyperbole.

When we achieve in one area of our life, deal with fears, and admit that we need help and support, then we can use the information over and over again. You see, preparation for one negotiation may very well become part of a knowledge base that will be used in future negotiations. At a minimum, greater knowledge will create increased confidence in future negotiations.

After a few weeks of preliminary preparation, Richard settled on a range of acceptable salary offers. He knew what others in his job category were paid and knew what friends in similar positions were paid in other companies. He realistically concluded that he couldn't possibly get parity with others in one jump. He knew enough about the company and its current financial status to realize that a raise would probably be modest. However, he also realized that his own contribution was considerable. In fact, he had managed to please a major customer whom others in his group had not been able to deal with effectively. He had also steadily increased the amount of business that regular clients did with the company.

Richard had been on the job so long that he had forgotten the value of his contributions. In any negotiation, your strengths are important to note and remember. This is the time to assess your resource inventory, those skills and experiences you have that will be called upon to negotiate effectively.

For example, if in the process of asking for a raise, Richard's boss mentioned the tight economy and the struggle to hang on to existing business, the fact that Richard's good work actually helped to retain a major client would be important information to mention. I've seen situations in which this kind of crucial knowledge turned the tide in a delicate negotiation process.

Richard was now ready to deal with some pre-negotiation factors, including setting and timing. Richard's boss was due to go on vacation in two weeks. Therefore, Richard had to either wait until he came back or approach him prior to his two week absence. There are many things to consider here.

Richard noticed that his boss was very tense while finishing up projects that had to be done before he left for his vacation. He barely had time to be cordial in the office. On the other hand, Richard knew that his boss often came back from a vacation with his family relaxed and for a few weeks he seemed like a new person. As eager as Richard was to resolve the matter, he decided to wait.

If you are thinking about situations that apply to your work life—and I hope you are—then you should note these details about the preparation for and the timing of a negotiation. What seems like a very long process for Richard was in reality a very carefully done preparation that ultimately created a scenario that worked to his advantage.

I must also tell you that Richard was not always on a clear course throughout these weeks of preparation. His fears returned from time to time and he even considered giving up his resolve to earn more money at his current job. He considered looking for a new job and starting fresh, though he enjoyed his current position very much. (This is not an irrational consideration; there are many situations that a person might be better off leaving.) However, Richard used his resources to address the fears as they came up—he stayed with his plan.

Richard knew that it was likely that he would be approaching his boss in the boss's office. He could propose a meeting through a memo or face to face on neutral ground, but the actual negotiation would be in the boss's "territory." In other situations, it's advantageous to plan to negotiate in your own space, but this was not possible in Richard's case.

There are advantages to negotiating on your own turf. First, you can control the environment, deciding whether to be interrupted and how you wish to be interrupted. Second, you have access to whatever materials or resources you might need to use. Finally, you have the psychological advantage of comfort since you know the space. On the other hand, the disadvantage to negotiating on your own turf is that you can't walk or storm out of your own space (well, not as easily as you can walk out of someone else's office).

On someone else's turf, you can't count on the other person producing whatever materials are needed if you forget to bring them with you. The other person can also be interrupted and you have no control over those interruptions or the comfort of the space.

Richard also had to determine if his proposal to his boss should be in writing, given to him before their meeting, or, whether it was advantageous to present it verbally at the time of the session. Deciding which is the better strategy may not be easy. When something is in writing, it has the advantage of being clear and there is a record of it. It can be read and thought about and be brought out later as a reference.

On the other hand, it may appear to be a final idea, one that is not flexible. It also gives the receiver of the proposal all the time he or she wants to review and consider the terms; time control is power, after all. Also, keep in mind that in some job situations, any proposal put in writing could be placed in that employee's file, which might not work to the employee's advantage later on in other salary or review situations.

Richard determined that he would approach his boss in person and ask for the raise orally. He would be prepared to discuss the issue either at length or, if the boss needed time to think and perhaps consult with other people, he would be brief. Richard also knew the boss fairly well, and if there was one thing that he hated, it was more paper to deal with. The boss was always more relaxed in conversation than when reviewing documents, and Richard's choice was probably wise.

Richard also knew that this kind of topic was one that his boss preferred to deal with at the end of the day rather than at the beginning. As you can see, Richard's process was sometimes detailed and precise. The subtleties of his boss's personality were even taken into consideration.

All of this mental preparation would never be wasted, no matter what the actual outcome of the negotiation. Why? Because Richard was carefully assessing his current situation and practicing his negotiation skills. He was learning the process, absorbing and synthesizing information that might be useful at another time for another purpose.

(As it turned out, Richard did use a similar thought process when he decided to approach his life partner about a family issue. He realized that timing and setting, plus gathering information were significant factors in keeping the give and take as pleasant as possible.)

A few days after his boss returned from his vacation, Richard requested a meeting with him. It was arranged through the secretary and put on the boss's calendar for two days after the request. Let's pretend that we can see how the negotiation went. We'll be flies on the wall and listen in. As we do, let's pay attention to the key factors of negotiation which emerge, including the control of information exchanged in the interaction, the use of principle to underlie each position stated, the desire to seek overlap between the needs of each person, and the balance of egos during the exchange.

Richard: Welcome back, sir. I made an appointment to discuss an important matter. Will this be a good time for you?

Mr. Nic: Sure, Richard. I'm just catching up on all the work that gathered while I was gone. How are you doing?

Richard: Just fine. Since you're busy, would you prefer I come back at another time?

Mr. Nic: Not at all. Let me put this work aside. Let's sit over there away from my desk and let me have my secretary hold my calls.

Here, Richard chooses not to rely on his boss's calendar obligations. He would (I think wisely) confirm that his boss is in a pleasant mood at this time. If not, Richard would be best advised to postpone the discussion until a later time. To do otherwise could jeopardize his potential success if his boss is not in a mood to listen. If this is a good time, then Richard has begun on the right foot with his boss, who is pleased at the respect shown to him. The clues here are important.

First, Mr. Nic indicates that he's busy. Richard was right to ask if he should come back. When Mr. Nic puts the papers aside, moves away from his desk and insures no interruptions, Richard can be certain he will have his boss's attention. Keep in mind that anything short of these steps may indicate the boss's resistance to the upcoming conversation.

Richard: Well, Mr. Nic, I'd like to ask you for your thoughts about my work product and whether you are satisfied with the work I am doing.

Mr. Nic: Absolutely! I am most pleased with you and your work. I believe you are one of the finest employees I have. Are you happy?

Richard: Well, yes, and I need to talk with your about my compensation. May we discuss the possibility of a merit raise for me?

Richard is wise to focus the discussion on Mr. Nic's evaluation of work product. By doing so, he begins to strengthen the position from which he will negotiate. Beginning with "I want a raise," will most likely be a turn off because it's a "want" statement and not an "the situation warrants" presentation. The latter adds support and substance.

Once Mr. Nic acknowledges Richard's excellent work product, Richard is in good position to approach the raise. His characterization of the raise as a "merit" raise also adds support; he is not looking for handouts. Rather, he makes it clear up front that he will base his request on the underlying facts.

Mr. Nic: Well, Richard, you know we have annual reviews. Your review isn't due for another six months. Why now?

Richard: You see, Mr. Nic, I have come to learn that other people in my same position both here and in other companies are making substantially more than I do. I don't want to do better than other people necessarily, but I do think my position warrants a higher salary. Since you agree that my work is good, I am hopeful that there is no reason not to put my salary at a level that is on a par with others in my same position.

Mr. Nic: Richard, the people in this company who make more than you have been here longer. They have more seniority. Your pay will match theirs in time.

Richard: I understand. Colleagues of mine in other companies with the same seniority are also at a higher pay level. I am not asking to move beyond seniority. I believe there is a happy medium that would put me where the position seems to be in other companies, and still gives those with more seniority their due here.

Mr. Nic: Well, let's explore that...

This negotiation is going to move along well because both Richard and Mr. Nic are focusing on the merits of the issue, and not on personalities. Comments like "You're unfair," or "You just don't get it," are personal attacks which won't get anyone very far. Richard is professional and proper to present underlying support and factual information to keep the discussion focused. Mr. Nic reacts appropriately.

If you negotiate with someone who begins to level personal attacks, it's essential that you refocus them on the issues. Use phrases such as, "Hey, let's not get personal. Let's just talk about the facts and explore creating a position that can work for both of us." Conversations that get personal quickly disintegrate into argument. (You no doubt know what I mean.) No one wins at that point.

Understand that both Richard and Mr. Nic were performing during the negotiation—not in a true theatrical sense, of course. But nevertheless, both people recognize that they have a role to fulfill, a role with a set of expectations and limitations. Richard needs to remember that he is in the role of "employee," which means that he needs to be respectful. Mr. Nic is in the role of boss, but also a support figure for employees. If you ever find yourself in a discussion that degenerates into argument, it may be because you have stepped outside of your expected role. Children who show disrespect for parents, employees who don't respect bosses, anyone of lesser status who insults someone of higher status, all face the consequences of role violation.

Looking at their styles, we can see that Richard exhibited the qualities of a cooperative negotiator and Mr. Nic was prepared to listen. A competitive negotiator might have begun to fight off the bat— Mr. Nic: "Look Richard, you're nothing special. You'll make what everyone else makes at your seniority level."

This is the sign of someone focusing on personality and not on underlying principle or issues. Competitive negotiators will focus on insults and ignore principle-based positions. Cooperative negotiators will focus on relationships and try to find areas of mutual agreement. Although it may at times be easier to work with cooperative negotiators, it is possible to work with a competitive negotiator by attempting to keep the focus where it is better placed, on positions.

Notice how the negotiation proceeded through a series of phases. First, Richard and Mr. Nic oriented and positioned the other as to timing and location. Next they began to state positions and to provide underlying support for those positions. As the negotiation proceeds, each will begin to examine the position of the other, asking questions to clarify what is said or proposed, and supporting their own positions. Eventually, adherence to each position through a phase of competition is replaced by a cooperative tone working towards resolution.

Conflict is natural in negotiation. It can help to clarify differences, and relationships can grow once each person understands what the other person is looking for in the discussions. You have to work to keep the conversation focused on the positions and off of the personalities of the players.

In the end, Richard may or may not achieve his raise at this time, but the discussion will progress with focus on needs and goals. Comments remain focused on the principles stated and are not directed at the people in a personal way.

We can't underestimate the importance of what Richard did for himself in this situation. He reinforced a relatively recent conviction that he could take charge of his life, and that practicing negotiation skills added quality to his life. No longer stuck in past patterns, he was now able to apply this knowledge elsewhere. He relied on the quality concepts, including a recognition of his talent from the basepoint and a reliance on his resource inventory.

For Richard, other people in similar positions gave him information to assist in this negotiation. Support from friends who encouraged him to proceed became a resource used to work through the process. Knowing what research needed to be done was also part of the resources Richard had available as he entered the negotiation.

Imagine the results and the nature of the interaction absent the use of these resources, or without considering all of the experiences and knowledge Richard had as part of his basepoint. The conversation would have been very different, and much less rewarding (putting it mildly).

This is why quality mind–quality life concepts are so exciting. When you understand it, you will see that it is a system that affects every part of your life. You may not even be aware of the connections and the many subtle changes you effect. But one day, you will realize, like Richard, that you have demanded quality of yourself and others around you. In Richard's case, he had more respect for himself, which resulted in others having more respect for him. Mr. Nic never levels an attack at Richard. Rather, he appears to respect an employee who shows him respect, and who bases his request in fact and foundation.

Take a minute now to think of the times you have negotiated something that made a difference in your life. List the opportunities that arise in your day-to-day life. You may find that your job involves this give and take many times a day. And, don't forget the kinds of negotiation that occur in your personal life. We use the professional example, and begin our discussion of the skills we need for a quality mind, simply because in my experience, so many people want to start life changes by altering work situations. But, the same skill you have just watched Richard develop is going to be used in every area of life.

No long ago, I saw a couple negotiate a good price for a condo they wanted to purchase. What should have been a clear cut offer and acceptance ended up being complicated by some damage done by flooding. The current owner's possessions were ruined, and the couple showed compassion as they renegotiated the terms of the contract. The owner was so upset by what had happened to her that the deal might have been scratched. The situation might have even ended up in a courtroom with each party claiming whatever rights and obligations served their purposes. However, goodwill prevailed, and both parties ended up with a quality deal. A sense of what is right plus skill in using the tools of negotiation led to resolution in this case.

I also want you to evaluate some missed opportunities in which negotiating skills could have helped you. Maybe you were intimidated and didn't choose to negotiate. Perhaps you didn't know how to go about setting up a negotiating session. Perhaps you tried, but you didn't do it well, and you missed out on something. Remember now, you are assessing these past situations only for the purpose of learning from them. You are dredging up the past in order to understand through reflection and honest self-evaluation.

What can you learn from that previous experience? What have you learned from this chapter that might have helped you in earlier situations in your life? Is there something going on at your workplace right now in which some negotiating might be in order?

Negotiations often involve money, but that is taking a narrow view. Maybe you want to negotiate a family leave, or shortened work hours, or more hours to provide some overtime salary. You may want to negotiate the terms of a new position with the same company. A friend of mine recently negotiated with his supervisor about doing some of his work at home. He was able to get a trial period, with specific goals that had to be met. He didn't win the boss over, but he did win the opportunity to try out this new work arrangement. That's what we're talking about when we use negotiation to bring quality into our lives.

We continue to negotiate all day long and in a variety of circumstances. As the work day comes to an end, we head home where we attempt to keep our personal lives in balance. When we negotiate situations at home we are often called upon to make many different types of decisions. Some may be big and involve a decision to have a child or change careers, decisions that can result in changes for the whole family. Other decisions are small by comparison—what television program to watch or whether to repair the old dishwasher or buy a new one.

The ability to communicate, manage conflict, and negotiate will be used in all settings, including how we make decisions. So, let's look at how we can make better decisions and see how this skill adds quality to our lives and brings us closer to those we love and with whom we want to get along well. We'll also see the way in which we can make our decisions and then handle situations in which others try to influence us. Who knows? By the time you're done, you might be well on your way to creating a new life.

CHAPTER VII

Achieving Balance in Decision-making:
Logic, Emotion, and A Quality Life

YOU MAKE MANY DECISIONS EACH DAY and have made hundreds of thousands of decisions in your life. Perhaps you don't think of the many small choices you make day in and day out as decisions, but they are. Decisions are not only those big choices, the ones that have an obvious and significant impact on your life. The small choices are important too. Insignificant as they seem at the time, they can have consequences and can affect the quality of your life.

If you began to put a lot of time and effort into every decision you make, you'd have little time left for implementing anything you ultimately decide to do! You'd be spending almost all your mental energy on issues of little consequence.

With all of the decisions we make on a day-to-day basis, it's useful to identify a pattern or system we appear to create each time we make a choice for our future. This chapter will help you uncover the process you go through each time you make a decision. By highlighting that process, the steps will create a new sense of confidence and ease as you make your choices in the future. And, by the way, you *always* have choices, no matter how much it might look as if you don't. But as you will see, good decision-makers are usually adept at identifying the range of choices they have.

As you work with quality mind–quality life ideas, you will find yourself thinking more about your choices and weighing all the pros and cons of each decision. Don't forget that decision-making ability

---

is an integral part of a quality mind. It fits within the overall system and becomes integrated into everything you do. After all, life is a series of ongoing choices. The art of decision-making is one of the most important skills you will ever develop.

Indecision, Power, and Anxiety

"I never make decisions," Angela says with regret in her voice. "I start, but I just don't finish the process, and it always seems as if life just happens." Angela is correct. People who don't make decisions for themselves are subject to the expectations and demands of others.

Life does just "happen" to them; they go along with whatever others decide and they have little or no control over their futures. The indecisive person invariably feels powerless and anxious; this is not a pleasant thought, but it is so true of too many people. If we look at Angela's life, we can see where indecisiveness has lead.

Angela is 41 years old, and has recently lost her job in a large corporation. She worked for this company for ten years, moving up the ladder as others left, but never discussing her career path with department managers or even close friends. For several years, she listened to rumor after rumor that downsizing was in the company's future plans.

Other people in Angela's department were let go, increasing the workload for those who were left (including Angela) and making it an unpleasant place to work. Almost every day, Angela thought about the possibility of losing her job, but she put that thought aside. As soon as the possibility occurred to her, she would begin to feel apprehensive.

It was easier to ignore her fear, and she succeeded at that much of the time. (If this sounds familiar, rest assured it's a common reaction, one that we could almost include in the category of "magical thinking," that is: If I don't think about something then I can ward it off. If I ignore a problem, it will disappear.)

Every now and then, Angela would daydream about what she really wanted to do. She would attempt to take her own destiny in hand. Sometimes she thought that she had too many choices, but at other times, she believed she had too few. Angela never took charge of her own career, and one day, the proverbial "pink slip" came. Her department was being phased out, and she was given an exit package based on her years of service. No matter how many times Angela had thought about this day coming (or avoided thinking about it), it still came as a shock to her.

Angela's pattern of indecisiveness is clear when you look at how she handled most decisions in her life. All she needed to do was honestly study the decisions she made in each area of her life. For example, she had been involved in a less than satisfactory relationship with a man, who one day said, "I'm leaving. This just isn't working." Angela wasn't surprised. In fact, she was relieved, but she hadn't taken any steps prior to that time to resolve the situation on her own. She simply reacted when the inevitable happened.

When she asked herself what she wanted out of life, Angela was able to talk only in vague generalities. She wanted to be happy, or she wanted to have what she called "peace of mind." But the nagging fears about her job and the nagging dissatisfactions about her relationship were two major obstacles to the very happiness and peace of mind she said she wanted.

Angela (and people just like her) is what I call a "life drifter." She is indecisive because she feels powerless; she is fearful and anxious much of the time. She believes—on some level—that she has no control over her own destiny. Of course, she also feels powerless because she is indecisive. It's a vicious circle, and can be broken only by beginning to take charge of life situations, one by one by one by one.

When, for example, I decided that I wanted to do major on-camera work as a legal correspondent, I couldn't necessarily make that happen during the first week. But, I made other choices, one by one, that put me in the right place at the right time. If I'd decided to take a six-month sabbatical and study marine life in Tahiti, then my choice would have gone contrary to my goal. But my series of steps eventually led me to NBC and the role I played in media coverage of a celebrity trial. I say this to illustrate that once we establish our vision, explore our dreams, and set firm goals, our choices—the day-to-day decisions we make—can empower us and move us closer and closer to reaching our goals.

Most of us go through occasional periods in life during which we drift along, taking what comes our way, initiating little in the way of new ideas and goals. If we generally act in a decisive manner, then it is fair to look at these periods as temporary. These are times in which we are unconsciously shifting our outlook and our focus.

For example, there are periods during which many of us are "recovering" from times when we must use every ounce of our energy to reach a goal or get through a period of excessive stress. When Judy finished her master's degree, she seemed to have little energy to make new plans. After five or six months, she gradually recovered her energy and made some new goals. For the decisive, these interludes of drifting and moments of decision are quickly followed by a return to balance.

For Angela, a change of attitude is called for, but this change can't occur until she begins to study and understand her pattern of indecision. Practicing a new decision-making process will help her develop a new attitude grounded in a set of skills. If you find yourself drifting in at least some areas of your life, developing a quality mind attitude will help you break this cycle. You will learn to make and implement decisions more effectively, thereby giving you a sense of power over your life.

Indecision Generally Means, "I Don't Have Any Goals"

I have never met a person who had clear, strong goals but who was also indecisive. The reverse is also true. I have never seen an indecisive person with clear, strong goals. Angela had a vague idea about what she wanted. But, simply being happy or having peace of mind are not strong goals. These concepts are vague and hard to make concrete. To go back to our earlier chapters, a goal to be happy lacks vision. To be sure, Angela lacks vision for her life.

For example, what will make Angela happy? What are the trappings of happiness for Angela? For that matter, what is the framework within which happiness can occur for her? What does peace of mind mean to her? Does she mean that she wants a life free from worries? If so, Angela may be asking for the impossible.

Without definition or concrete language, goals remain vague and effective decision-making becomes virtually impossible. After all, if you don't have goals, what are you making decisions about? Yet, even the most indecisive among us make decisions, and in fact, make them every day. They just don't realize that they are exercising a skill. If you have labeled yourself "indecisive," then remember, you made a decision just by picking up this book. You made another decision when you opened it, and each time you start a new chapter you are making another decision.

If you are reading this book over breakfast this morning, you made several decisions, namely, to purchase the book, to have breakfast, and to use your breakfast time to continue your reading and create positive change in your life. So you see, you are not without the skill of decision-making, you just need to recognize and develop it. And you are already on your way.

Don't lose sight of vision and goals. First, we have a vision, a statement of what we're about; then we have goals in particular areas of our life. Your goals reflect your vision, and if that isn't the case, you reevaluate and try to make all the elements harmonious. Then, you have to make plans to implement your goals.

From the time we start forming a vision and stating our goals, we are involved in decision-making. Done in this way, however, we add a sense of direction and control that may have been lacking in all of our previous life decisions. It's easy to see why Angela characterized herself as not being effective at making good decisions. She didn't have any goals that could be planned for, and therefore, she avoided the mental process of making choices. She was doomed in the decision-making process from the very beginning.

Keep in mind that major life events—marriage, birth of a child, divorce, finishing degrees, recovering from serious illness, and so on, almost always require some "down time." If you find yourself in this kind of situation, be patient with yourself, particularly if you have always been a fairly decisive person in the past.

The kind of indecision we are talking about here, and which requires adjustment, is generally *chronic*—like Angela's. It usually affects almost every area of life, leaving the person feeling powerless and without direction. Goals, on the other hand, empower us, energize us, and by their very nature require us to be decisive. After all, you had to go through a decision-making process in order to set the goals in the first place.

It's Not For Lack of Experience

Remember, you have already made thousands of decisions throughout your life, so I am not talking about anything that isn't already a part of your daily routine. You decide what to eat and wear every day. You decide if you're going to run for the bus or wait for the next one. You decide to shift a work task to tomorrow rather than doing it today, consider whether to bring up a problem at the dinner table or keep it to yourself.

We decide to avoid certain small annoyances because we don't want to take the time—right now—to consider other choices. We constantly put some decisions on hold, make others immediately, look for new options in some cases, or weigh all the pros and cons in others.

While you may not have realized it, and we don't think about this as often as we should, our mental state is an important part of how we make these small daily decisions. You may go into the decision-making process with your mind already made up. As a result you have set the conclusion in motion. How often do you see that bus just up the street and decide, with the negative attitude in place, that: "I always miss that bus;" or "These buses always run late and now I'll be late for work." Perhaps before you take the first bite, breakfast is greeted with your mental thought, "I hate this cereal, but I have to eat it."

Consider how you would approach that same situation if, as you see the bus, you think: "If I walk just a bit faster, I bet I can catch that bus;" or "I still have time to spare, so I'll not risk spraining my weak ankle by running for this bus." Imagine sitting down to that same breakfast and noting, "There are so many choices in the store that as soon as I finish this box of cereal I think I'll try something new." When was the last time you arrived at work thinking, "I worked well yesterday, and I wonder what challenging task I'll have the opportunity to work on today."

The common theme in these thoughts is a simple shift in mental attitude from the inevitable negative to the hopeful positive. If you begin cultivating this way of thinking, the remarkable change will show itself in the difference in choices you begin to make. And don't forget, even the small choices count.

Each of our choices represents an opportunity for personal growth—that's the reality of it. For example, we may find ourselves having to make the "run for the bus or wait for the next one" choice many days in a row. If we blame other people—and the public transportation company—we don't bother to look at what we are doing to contribute to our own problem.

In short, we can make a different decision, and as a result, change the entire situation. What are the options? We can leave the house five minutes earlier, we can buy a car, we can move, we can look for a job closer to home. Are these choices extreme? Perhaps. But they do represent a range of options, many of which are ignored. Change begins by recognizing that staying the current course will produce the same problem day after day. It is amazing how easy it is for us to blame the bus driver, the weather, the office, the national economy, and everything else except ourselves.

Yet, probably 99 percent of the time, we can create positive change by deciding to leave a few minutes earlier—a simple change, not in the world, but in ourselves. This simple decision may lead to other small decisions about our morning routine that create a positive change. Going through the process of making the decision, we may find significant value in learning that change begins with us.

The last place we want to start is often the easiest and best place to begin. If missing the bus and getting to work late occur on a daily basis, isn't the situation resolved a bit easier once we consider how nice it would be to get an earlier start or even to walk to work?

What's stopping you? Candidly, it is too simplistic to think that we can completely change our lives just by recognizing and accepting responsibility for beginning to change by starting with ourselves. After all, personal change carries risk and consequences—and it takes time.

Effective decision-making is a product of balance and rational thinking. Consider most of the decisions we make. They result from impulse, or are made without thorough consideration, or are triggered from the heart, or are made because certain options stand above any other choices, whatever they may be. Quality decision-making means a search for all alternatives or choices in any given situation.

Quality decision-making also means using both your instinct and sense of rational thinking to evaluate each option. It means first uncovering all options before making any judgement about the value or utility of any one of them. It means selecting the best option only after all options have been carefully processed through the heart and mind. It means working to implement the option selected so a positive change results from a decision. It means taking the steps to produce that change.

This all seems so easy, but we generally don't make decisions quite that quickly, or nearly so effectively. It always harkens back to the same factors that can be summed up in one mind-blocking question: "What if?" Let's explore what we are afraid of in the world of "what if."

The Fret Factors: Risk and Consequence

Although it might not seem obvious at first, every decision involves some risk and carries a consequence. Whether we're talking about small decisions or the more monumental ones, we need to evaluate the factors of risk and consequence along the way. Consider a relatively small decision.

You may decide, on impulse, to buy a compact disk. But you realize that you are left a few dollars short when you look at your budget. You may then decide to take your lunch to work rather than eat out, in order to make up for the impulsive purchase. (It doesn't sound like such an impulsive decision anymore, does it?)

Imagine making that same impulsive purchase, but not having a clear budget against which to consider the impact of the decision, good or bad. You will not have an accurate idea of how these decisions will ultimately affect you and the quality factor in your life. Most of us do seem to recognize that we are always short of money. This is where our own personalities and other skill levels come into play. For example, one person must decide what to take for lunch; another person may need to decide to make a budget. No matter how large or small, all our decisions reflect who we are—our values, desires, material assets at the moment, tastes, needs, skills, and so on.

If we make decisions but don't think about the risks or the consequences, then we can't coordinate what changes we wish to make in our lives. We may even have trouble establishing goals. We simply haven't evaluated any of the elements. Part of effective decision-making is evaluating your personal goals and values in order to make decisions based on whether you are advancing, expressing, and living them.

When we have firmly established our goals and values and keep them foremost in our minds, we may find that many of our decisions are made easily and in a positive frame of mind. It is also easier to see the personal consequence of the decision as well as the need for making personal change.

For example, if you value your integrity and your impeccable business reputation, then you aren't likely to go along with a shady business deal in which one of your respected competitors will be hurt. Your own personal standards would be violated if you looked the other way, and you will simply say no. On the other hand, you may not be in the "power" position to call the shots in that situation. The decision may not be yours to make. In this case, the decision becomes more complex. You may find yourself struggling with the issues of knowledge versus personal responsibility.

Getting In Touch with Value

By this point in the book, you ought to have a fair sense of who you are and what you want. You have a vision and you are beginning, step by step, to create quality and balance within and without. However, in order to link the whole area of decision-making with your attitude and values, it is important to place what you value as part of a simple hierarchy. For example, a person such as Angela might decide that she really doesn't care very much about having a relationship. She may discover when she looks deeply inside herself that she would rather put emphasis on her career.

Don't be surprised to find your values and priorities changing at various times in your life. While career may be a prominent quality issue for you now, having a satisfying love relationship might become a priority quality issue later on. We will make decisions based on our present attitudes and thinking, but we will also bring in past experiences and future goals.

Following is a list of characteristics, defining qualities, life areas, drives, and attitudes that all of us have as part of what makes us unique. We can begin to define our values when we evaluate how important each is to us. Read down the list and think about the importance of each of these issues in your own life. Whatever value you assign to these factors is likely to be reflected in the decisions you make in life. In fact, consider how each of these factors comes into play when you consider and make each particular decision.

Evaluate each of the following and determine which are very important, somewhat important, reasonably important, somewhat unimportant, or of no importance.

- Physical health
- A love (intimate) relationship
- Relationship with family

- Money for living expenses
- Career
- Personal appearance
- Material possessions
- Money saved for emergencies or future luxuries
- Money saved for present and future security
- Education
- Religion
- Ethnicity
- Power and Prestige (visible to others)
- Personal power (whether visible to others or not)
- Hobbies or intellectual stimulation
- Creativity and the arts
- Solitude
- Social life—close friends
- Social life—social or casual acquaintances
- Political and social issues (causes and beliefs)
- Volunteering to help others
- Being a respected person

Clearly this list covers a variety of areas, some more important to you than others. Keep in mind that each person's evaluation will be unique. This is why people make different decisions, experience different consequences, and react differently to those consequences. For example, my friend Ben told me recently that he hadn't thought much about the ways in which his religion and his ethnic background had originally shaped him and continues to influence his values and decisions. But when asked to put it into a hierarchy, his religious beliefs and ethnicity were very important.

Other people might go through this exercise and find out that they really don't care about having money in order to participate in the great American material consumption game. They may realize that when they forget all the advertisements and the pressure to buy things, they really don't care very much about owning new items or living in a bigger house. Some people make certain decisions that result in particular kinds of clothing or a prestigious address. One day, they come to realize that they don't care about those things at all.

Quite to the contrary, other people have a deprivation mentality which leads them to talk about "making ends meet." However, they'd actually rather live more comfortably and have more luxury items. But, for some reason, they consistently make decisions that permit them to do little more than to make ends meet.

There are no right or wrong answers here, but give yourself some time to come up with a profile—a narrative description of what you value most. You may find that you change more than you know just by considering the factors set out above. In certain stages in life, we may value power and prestige more than at other times. We may find that we want the respect and admiration of others at certain points, because we are trying to break into new fields or are attempting to climb a specific career ladder.

Take some time to create a chart of the values that affect you and consider their relative importance for you. The above list of values is not exhaustive, so feel free to add other factors that occur to you and are affecting your decision process.

Decision Values Evaluation

Decision Situation:

Value Factor	Importance Rating	Comments
Physical health		
Love (intimate) relationship		
Relationship with family		
Money for living expenses		
Career		
Personal appearance		
Material possessions		
Money for emergencies/ luxuries		
Money for security		
Education		
Religion		
Ethnicity		
Power and Prestige		
Personal power		
Hobbies/intellectual stimulation		
Creativity/arts		

Solitude

Social life (close friends)

Social life (social/casual
  acquaintances)

Political/social issues
  (causes and beliefs)

Volunteering to help
  others

Being a respected person

Let's see how Angela might complete this form for her decision situation:

Decision Values Evaluation

Decision Situation:

Value Factor	Importance Rating	Comments
Physical health	Very Important	I'm in excellent physical condition
Love (intimate) relationship	Not Very Important	Just out of a bad relationship
Relationship with family	Somewhat Important	Can take some family members and leave some
Money for living expenses	Very Important	Need security
Career	Somewhat Important	
Personal appearance	Very Important	Spend money on good clothes and a health club
Material possessions	Not Very Important	Don't shop much

Money for emergencies/ luxuries	Important	Need security more than luxuries
Money for security	Very Important	Don't want to be a "bag lady"
Education	Not Important	Have done that in the past
Religion	Not Very Important	Haven't thought about it much
Ethnicity	Somewhat Important	Big Italian family with lots of rituals—love them
Power and Prestige	Not Important	Don't even consider that when making decisions
Personal power	Don't know	Don't know exactly what it means
Hobbies/intellectual stimulation	Somewhat Important	Always curious about the world
Creativity/arts	Somewhat Important	Make time to cook gourmet meals
Solitude	Very Important	Happy alone with a video or a book
Social life (close friends)	Somewhat Important	Haven't felt like participating much lately
Social life (social/casual acquaintances)	Not Important	Have only close friends
Political/social issues (causes and beliefs)	Somewhat Important	Spend time keeping up
Volunteering to help others	Somewhat Important	Used to do much more, have drifted away
Being a respected person	Somewhat Important	Don't think about it much

So, what do we know about Angela, and more important, what did Angela learn about herself? The first thing she said was, "I hadn't stopped to think about how much I'd been focused on my bad relationship and unconsciously worrying about my job. I've neglected to give much thought to so many things."

We know that Angela doesn't care very much about personal power, because she hadn't given it much thought—besides, she'd turned over much of her own autonomy to the man she had been involved with. She also hadn't developed new interests or friendships, and in fact, hadn't participated in an active social life for some time.

Again, this could be the result of her less than fine relationship. We do know that Angela is a gourmet cook who identifies with her large Italian family, some of whom she enjoys and some of whom she doesn't. She has an active, curious mind and cares about the issues of the day, and in the past, she had spent time as a volunteer.

We can see just how indecision about one area of life can affect everything else. Angela essentially told us that there are a few things she consciously considers at least somewhat important—her physical health, her appearance, financial security, her family, some creative expression, and her intellectual interests. But she also had a hard time even responding to issues involving action and moment by moment decisions. She is probably not alone in these areas.

How often have you considered if being a respected person is important to you? Do you even consider your actions in relation to how much respect they will bring or whether they are leading you toward a sense of personal power?

Like many people, Angela hadn't thought much about prestige. She was simply trying to hang on to her job, cope with a bad relationship, and spend quiet time at home. When she did spend time and money, it seems as if she used it to "keep up appearances"—literally. Fortunately, Angela is an independent spirit and has a willingness to reevaluate her life.

People Who Need People... The Unconscious Roadblock

We rarely make decisions in a vacuum. Other than our small daily decisions, almost every major choice we make will have an impact on other people in our life, from our life partner and close friends to our coworkers or employees—even to the community at large.

Take a few minutes to examine the relationships in your life. Answer the following questions and you will reveal to yourself much valuable information you may currently be overlooking as you make decisions.

- Who are the most significant people in your life? Do you live with these people? Are you dependent on them for certain material things? Nonmaterial things? Are they dependent on you for material or nonmaterial things?

- Who do you believe has the most influence or power on the way you choose to lead your life? How do you feel about these individuals and the position they hold in relation to you? Are these satisfactory relationships? Is change needed in the dynamics between you and any of these individuals?

- Who do you influence or have power over? What kind of power or influence is it? That is, is it your responsibility to have influence over them, or have you taken this on for reasons you can't define? (If you have young children, for example, it is your responsibility to influence them as well as meet their dependency needs.) How do you exercise this power? As a dictator, or with dialogue and evaluation?

- Who are the people you seek for advice and guidance? Why do you want them in your life? What do they do for you and what do you do for them? What qualities do you admire in them? What values do they have that you share or want to develop in yourself?

- Are there people in your life to whom you have turned over important decisions? In other words, are there situations in which you let others make the ultimate choice? Why do you do this? Out of necessity or by free choice? Do you believe they had power over you? Are you afraid to stand on your own? Which people turn their decisions over to you? What do they want from you?

What kind of decision resource profile did you begin to create? Barry, an acquaintance of mine, found that he spent very little time with the people he says he cares about, but ended up squandering time with people that matter little to him. "I haven't called my sister Jan in months," Barry says, "yet I say that having a close family is important to me. My uncle Gus has been a guiding force in my life, helping me choose a college and a career, but now I say little more than hello to him at large family gatherings. I've made some odd choices, but I haven't made any useful decisions about how I can best use my time; the day fills before I know it."

Barry is not an uncaring person, he just hasn't made the most beneficial or growth-producing decisions. In fact, what happened to Barry can happen to all of us when we don't take control of our activities and schedule our time around what we value. Barry's experience is the purpose that underlies this brief exercise. We can't make good decisions if we don't know what we want to make decisions about and which people are best included in that process.

Being There is the Next Best Thing to Avoidance

No one exercises his or her decision-making power 100 percent of the time. For example, take a moment to consider a decision situation that you avoided in the past. Perhaps, like Angela, you avoided making an appropriate career move. Or, like my friend Sam, you may have avoided making a relationship decision and ended up losing the other person. Maybe you avoided a health-related decision and suffered a consequence later on.

How much time did you spend considering the choices you had? Did you avoid thinking about your choices, or did you agonize over them, but still not make a decision and a commitment to one choice? Were there other people who would have been affected by whatever decision you made?

Certainly Sam's indecision affected his partner, who ultimately left him and sought another relationship—with someone who knew what he wanted. Angela's decision didn't directly affect others, which added to her sense that it didn't really matter much what she did. A delayed decision about a health problem could have an impact on many, many people. Evaluate the decision you avoided by answering some of these questions.

Next, try to determine why you avoided the decision. Were you afraid of a negative consequence? Were you afraid of how others would react? Did you need to involve someone else in the decision but didn't take the necessary steps to do so? Did you think that the decision would work itself out, thereby enabling you to avoid a choice?

Now, consider what the consequences were of not making the decision. Some outcomes might have been positive—list those, too. But, chances are, you have chosen this "non-decision" precisely because it hurt you in some way. Can you think about the benefits that you would have enjoyed had you acted decisively? Both Angela and Sam are able to name specific benefits they missed because they avoided making a choice about their lives.

In fact, as part of this exercise, I asked them to evaluate how their lives would have been different had they made a choice when they had the opportunity. In both cases, they envisioned their lives as better if they had made a decision. Angela believed that she would have had a better job, perhaps one in a field she liked more, and Sam believed that he lost out on a very good chance for happiness because he was afraid to make a commitment.

As you conduct your own evaluation, be gentle with yourself, and focus on what you can learn from the past process. You are now creating a quality life, and if you have found that decision-making has not been one of your strongest skills in the past, that is about to change.

Is the Road There if You Don't See it? You Bet: Uncovering Options

Once Angela lost her job, she had to face facts. She had to work. That was a given in her life. So, as part of her resolve to change her life, it was time to put herself in the frame of mind to make a decision. As Angela said, "I could have chosen to find the first available job in my field [corporate communications] and been happy to get it. But I decided to try to make some significant changes in my life. Trouble is, I don't know what to do first."

In situations such as Angela's, in which a decision requires time and its consequences are far reaching, the first step is *always* to evaluate options. No matter how locked in most of us feel, there are always options. Because Angela had not been through this structured process, I suggested that she brainstorm in order to open up her creative channels. Other people bypass this process because they are more skilled and, therefore, more comfortable in making decisions.

I'll let you get an inside look into Angela's process. I worked with her in a small group and others were invited to help her brainstorm. Here is a sample of the options Angela had. Remember, *everything* was put on the table. Nothing was censored or judged at the time; this is the essence of brainstorming. The pruning process came later.

Angela and the group free-wheeled the following options:

- Work a temp job until she found exactly what she wanted
- See a career counselor to explore new fields
- Leave town and look for a job in a geographic area that had more appeal
- Accept a job offer in a family business that involved selling home furnishings
- Use the exit package money to open her own business
- Use the exit money to vacation for a few months and think more about what she wanted
- Polish up her resume and begin looking at a dozen top companies that had good communication departments
- Invest in an apartment building and live off the small income
- Immediately cut back all her expenses in order to conserve her resources
- Go away for two weeks to a family cottage and do nothing
- Go back to school and get a new degree in the computer field

This process was quite unnerving for Angela, because although she had not been active in changing her life and making *proactive* decisions or setting goals, neither had she ever just done nothing, or spent money without knowing where her resources would come from or how they would arrive. At first, she rejected any suggestion that she sit back to think about these options.

By the time the evening with Angela was over, she had decided to look for a temporary job and cut back her expenses. She was comfortable with that decision because it bought her some time without leaving her in a state of financial insecurity. In short, she could save her exit package money but leave some options open. This decision cannot be made without first reviewing all the options, once they are all put on the table, and searching for the best alternative.

Many people find it easier to evaluate options when they set out all the positive and negative consequences of each possibility. Use the following chart to track the way you consider each decision option.

Options Evaluation

Decision Situation:

Option	Advantages	Costs Overall
1.		
2.		
3.		
4.		
5.		
6.		
7.		
8.		
9.		
10.		

Let's see how Angela completed this form for her decision situation:

Options Evaluation

Decision Situation:

Option	Advantages	Costs Overall
1. temp job	some money/security	only time – a possibility
2. career counselor	explore new things	approx. $600 – not appealing
3. relocate	fulfilling a deep wish	20% of exit – positive gut reaction
4. family business	security	low salary – Ho Hum
5. start business	independence	40% exit $ – a sense of excitement
6. vacation	rest/relax	too high to justify – not a good idea
7. job hunt	security	negligible – Ho Hum
8. buy a building –	buying time	80% of exit $ – too scary
9. cut back expenses	prudent/wise	N.A. – okay, not exciting, but wise
10. 2 wks at cottage	time to think	nominal – tempting
11. school	increase marketability	30% of exit $ – Ho Hum

There's No Harm in Thinking

After six weeks of working a temp job, Angela called me and reported that she had decided to go to her family's cottage on the shores of a lake in Wisconsin, and do nothing except think and consider her options for two weeks. She had put a time-frame around making some decisions, which in this case, was likely a wise choice, since not deciding was something she was all too comfortable doing (or not doing). She had been stuck in indecision so many times that assigning a deadline to this decision to take another step made sense to her.

At this point, Angela's decisions could be called "stop-gap" choices, because she had yet to form concrete goals. Notice that, uncomfortable as it was, Angela was pushing herself, and the stop-gap measures did not lack quality. The "old" Angela would have kept putting off a choice until the money was gone. The new Angela put a series of steps into place.

When Angela came back from her two-week hiatus, she had decided to move to a new area and set up her own communications business. The others in the group were amazed at her ability to make these choices when she had seemed so timid before. However, while Angela was away, two important things happened. First, she realized how much she dreaded the thought of working for still another corporation. Second, she realized that, with a bad relationship out of her life, she had the freedom to move to an area that had long appealed to her and where she also has a close friend.

It's amazing the way decisiveness can propel more action. Angela made a list of things she had to do to accomplish her move. There were still more questions to ask, more time-frames to set up, and many arrangements to make. Angela was thrust into many small and large decision-making situations as a consequence of her decision to act. She had to decide what belongings to take with her and which to sell or give away. She had to plan for her new business—a daunting job in the best of situations. She decided to make the move in six weeks, giving her a chance to more properly plan for the upcoming change.

As Angela's moving date grew closer, she realized that opening a business would be too big a task to take on when she first arrived in the medium-size city. So, she took the pressure off herself by resolving to find temp jobs in her new town before she went out on her own. It was important for Angela to maintain a degree of flexibility throughout the entire process. We can often encounter obstacles or barriers that are unknown at the time of the decision. Keep an open mind and sense of flexibility to adjust your decision path accordingly.

As I talked with Angela, I could see that she was thinking these problems through very carefully, and I asked her if she was avoiding making a decision about her business, or whether she was making the choice to delay the business in a considered way. In order to keep herself from drifting into another unsatisfactory job, Angela made a list of steps that she would need to take in order to open the new business. Her list included everything from joining professional associations to evaluating office equipment to researching the companies that might use independent contractors for their communications needs.

She also began to see her skills as elastic and transferable. If she could write internal newsletters and corporate reports, couldn't she also write marketing materials and client newsletters? She began to define herself as a business writer. And so the effective decision-making process continued.

I reminded Angela to put contingency plans in place wherever possible; again, flexibility is the key to effective decisions in a less than perfect anticipated world. What would she do if she couldn't find a temp job? How much money would she have to live on each month if she didn't find a job? How long would her exit money last? Would she live with her friend for a week or six months? What would she do if her car broke down?

When I last talked to Angela, she was working part-time as a word processor in a medical office. Temp jobs were not as plentiful in her new town as they had been in Chicago. She had never planned to live with her friend for a long period of time, but the friend was able to find her a small coach house that had stood empty for a year. The owner was glad just to have someone staying in it, keeping it up and preventing it from deteriorating. The rent was very low, and the job covered her basic expenses.

This was clearly a win–win (and quality) arrangement for both Angela and her landlord. She had just landed her first freelance writing job, and was going to an interview for another. Angela also noticed, as many people do when they begin to take charge of their lives, that she had less apprehension in this supposedly insecure life than she had when she was working in a big company. The options you have when making your decision may not be obvious or even particularly appealing, but when you look at them, be sure to give each some attention. The best way to develop decision-making skills is to go through the process consciously. Also keep in mind that you don't have to evaluate each option immediately after generating as many options as you can think of. If the situation permits, let some days or even weeks pass before evaluating the options. Our minds have the ability to see consequences and make comparisons if the pressure we are under is reduced. Time pressure is one of the worst enemies to an effective decision.

The Heart-Mind Connection: Seeking Balance

"I try to make sensible decisions," Joseph said, "but my emotions keep getting in the way." He expresses an attitude common among many people. Some people believe that if a particular choice arouses good anticipatory feelings, then the decision must be a bad one. (This must be one of legacies of Puritanism. If it feels good, it must be bad for you.) It's simply not true that we must push our emotions aside in the face of selecting among choices.

Our emotions are part of our "gut" responses that often guide us in our best actions. We say that something "felt right," or "felt wrong." Few of us can say that we have always followed these gut instincts, and many times we wish we had. Our gut instincts often serve us well when we are evaluating our options.

For example, when she first lost her job, Angela thought that she probably should polish up her resume, put on her best suit, and get as many interviews as possible. But every time she thought about doing that, something told her that it just wasn't the right thing to do. The two weeks of "time out" at the cottage helped her clarify her feelings and maintain perspective on the decision situation.

But, Angela didn't make her choice on gut reaction alone. She evaluated the emotional reaction she had against the other options. She realized that she had more than one choice, and before she went off and lived out a "should" reaction, she took time to *think*, to *weigh* the possible consequences, to *evaluate* her emotional response to all her choices. Welcome a sense of rational logic as part of evaluating options.

One of the people in the group asked Angela to think about the worst thing that could happen as a result of her ultimate choice. Angela considered that and recognized that the worst case scenario was that she could end up not being able to make a go of the business and not like the new town either. So, what would she do then? "Well, Angela said, "I can save enough money to move back here and see if I can work in the family business long enough to settle down again."

We will have different worst case scenarios, and we will all have different contingency plans. What we decide and how we evaluate always goes back to our values and the relative importance of the decision components pointed out earlier. If Angela didn't have a family business to consider, she might have had to think about something else.

As it happened, Angela loved the new town and had decided to stay there even if her business didn't succeed. At that point, she would have to make a new decision about a job. The process Angela went through was a very logical one as well as one guided by her emotional responses. The balance was the key.

What happened to Angela is not that unusual for people who have made a balanced decision. For a person who had made few choices in life, it seemed that she made some important decisions that had important consequences. But, the point is, she was willing to face the negative consequences and didn't let the fear of them deter her from her goal. Lest you forget, this is the same Angela who had no goals when I first met her.

It can't be emphasized enough how decision-making and goals go together. Angela became a skilled decision maker because she took charge of the important decision components affecting her life.

Finding the Rainbow

Some people think about benefits of particular options in terms of pay-offs; these people like to keep track of the balance of pay-offs. Although Angela might have said that the pay-off she got from her move was the chance to live in a new town and try a business, there were other pay-offs, though perhaps not as obvious.

I can guarantee that even if the worst happened, and Angela had to come back to her "old world," she would still have experienced enormous personal growth. She would have had an adventure, learned something about organization, planning, and above all, decision-making. As it turned out, Angela had drive and ambition that she hadn't yet begun to unleash. (She thought, and I agreed, that the less than satisfactory relationship was part of her low self image. Lack of quality in one area spilled over into another.)

We all make decisions based on future pay-offs over both big and small issues. We make the decision to buy a coat because we need it for warmth. Which coat we buy may be based on other things, such as image, comfort, utility, or design. We may want a coat that enhances our professional image. A coat selected for warmth alone may produce an overall negative pay-off if it fails to meet any other need that also ranks as important somewhere, either consciously or unconsciously.

I know one person who resolved this issue by buying a coat at an up-scale resale store. Warmth and image were combined. This particular person felt great about his choice because he had a sense that he "beat the system." He needed a certain kind of coat and didn't have the money for it, but he found a way to bring the quality he needed into his situation. That's a good example of a creative quality mind, a decision involving an effective balance in emotion and logic.

No two people will have the same choices to make, and no two people will have the same set of pay-offs. I know people who would do just about anything to avoid wearing anything second hand. That's their choice, but are they making an effective decision, or are they just going on the automatic pilot of old habit?

There are people, for example, who won't try a new food, go to a particular kind of movie, or read a certain magazine because they have never done it before, or perhaps did not enjoy it in the past. But, once they begin to open up to the options available to them, they begin, little by little, to bring new experiences into their lives.

We could argue that it doesn't matter much if we refuse to see certain kinds of movies or eat a particular cuisine. But, it can also be argued that when we make decisions about the small things, and evaluate our comparatively small choices, it helps us make better big ones. As I said, Angela will never be the same again. She took a risk, evaluated her options, and thought out the pay-offs, both positive and negative. This just has to spill over to her future decisions. Would you not agree?

Swing and Follow Through

Any golfer will preach the importance of following through. Perhaps nothing is more important to the decision-making process than ensuring proper implementation of the selected course of action. In its simplest terms, what use is uncovering every decision choice, carefully evaluating each option, selecting the option of most utility, and then *not* following through to bring the decision to fruition. It all becomes a wasted endeavor, does it not? Yet, so many people fall short in the decision-making process because they cannot find the way to make their decision choice a reality.

Once you have exercised every sense of rational and emotional processing to select the choice with the most appropriate outcome, it is essential to establish the means by which you will carry out the choice.

The simplest way to accomplish this is by creating an implementation plan. Your plan should set out the specific steps necessary to establish complete implementation. Sub-divide the components so that they are as small as possible; the smaller the task, the more manageable it is and the more likely it becomes that you will implement each step.

Next, set a time or date by which each step will be completed. This establishes a workable guide and a measurement tool to ensure that you remain on course. Of course, if there is a date set for the choice to be implemented as a whole, then start at that end date and work backwards to insure a reasonable amount of time for each preceding step. If you find that there is insufficient time to complete all steps, then you will need to re-evaluate the total amount of time allotted for implementation to determine whether it was workable in the first place. If you should learn that a choice cannot be implemented by an externally imposed deadline, you may find this awakens you to return to the decision selection process and choose another alternative. Once again, never lose your sense of flexibility in the process.

Following is a sample implementation form you might use to subdivide your task.

Implementation Schedule

Decision Choice:

Completion Date:

Task	Values Affected	Completion Date	Check when task is completed
1.			
2.			
3.			
4.			
5.			
6.			
7.			
8.			
9.			
10.			

Let's take a look at how Angela might complete the implementation schedule for her decision:

Implementation Schedule

Decision Choice: Moving to Appealtown

Completion Date: July 1, 1995

Task	Values Affected	Completion Date	Check when task is completed
1. closing up apartment	security	June 30, 1995	☐
2. what to take/what to leave behind	security	June 15, 1995	☐
3. buying a car	adjusting to a new way of life	June 15, 1995	☐
4. saying good-bye to family and friends	closure and decisions about what and who are important in my life	June 30, 1995	☐
5. arranging for move: move myself and get my own truck or hire a mover	important to conserve funds; like the idea of paring down enough to load truck myself with help of friend's teenage son; found I anticipate sense of freedom of not carrying around a lot of needless "stuff"	July 1,1995	☐
6. make temp contacts before move	establish a sense of having something to do immediately	June 1, 1995	☐
7. lay ground rules with friend prior to arriving	love my friend and don't want to wear out welcome	June 15, 1995	☐
8. establish budget for move	worry about money	May 15, 1995	☐

9. put business matters in order, get letters of recommendation, arrange for easy transfer of funds from bank to bank, notify financial institutions of change of address, make sure medical records are in order	be sure of things working as smoothly as possible	June 24, 1995	☐

Angela made her list in the presence of our group and she added items and tasks in the order in which she thought of them. In the process of making a list, individual decisions popped up for her to tackle, some of which she handled on the spot.

For example, she might have assumed that the only possible way to move was to hire a moving company. But, when she thought about the expense, it occurred to her then and there that her friend's son could easily help her and if she pared her belongings down, she could save money and move herself. Besides, her friend had room for only a small number of Angela's belongings, most of which would be stored in the basement.

As it turned out, Angela decided against buying a car before she left, and her friend initiated the discussion of the ground rules. Our group learned of Angela's decision before her family did, and the next week we heard of the horrified reaction of some relatives, including her father and two of her four sisters. They were shocked, told her that she couldn't go off to live among strangers, and who did she think she was to make such a decision without consulting them? Angela's father was sure he had convinced her to give up the idea, and she admitted that he was a very powerful figure in her life.

Angela's situation illustrates why it is sometimes advantageous to talk about visions, goals, life plans, and decision-making with people other than those who are closest to us. Too often, they are invested in our decisions. They may genuinely care about us, but they may have an agenda for us that is not compatible with what we have decided we want.

In other words, even the most well-meaning people can sabotage what is best for us—what we *know* to be best for us. Out of seven children, only Angela had ever even proposed moving away from the Chicago area and hence, away from their parents. Angela's sisters tried guilt; Angela's father tried using patriarchal power. Much to the dismay of the rest of the family, only Angela's mother quietly said that even though she didn't like it, she supported her choice. In our group, we all breathed a sigh of relief when Angela reaffirmed her intention to move.

If You Agree So Far, New Decisions Begin Today

Pick a day or a week or a month and keep track of all the decisions you make during that time. List them all, large and small. Evaluate how you make them, what your options are, and what pay-offs may result. Stretch these decision-making muscles, if you will, and bring your consciousness into all your choices. Involve others whom you respect or who might be affected by the decision choice you make.

Eventually, you will develop a new habitual pattern of decision-making, but you may find in your new awareness of the process, that you are now making all decisions, both small and big, in a more considered, careful way, and achieving the proper balance between emotion and logic.

Angela is a dramatic example of what happens when we decide to take charge. Use her as an example of the way in which life can be turned around and control can be regained. Your quality life depends on it.

You have seen Angela make major changes in her life in part because she improved her decision-making skills. But, to implement her decisions, Angela needed to stay focused and organized. She also had to manage her time in order to pull together all the details of her major life changes—and to keep her from becoming over-stressed by the process. In the next chapter, we'll discuss the ways in which essential organizational skills and managing both time and stress can help you balance your life.

CHAPTER VIII

Stress, Time, and Organization

STRESS IS ONE OF THOSE THINGS that no one knows exactly how to define, but we sure know it when we see it—or feel it. We throw the word stress around rather loosely these days, and people tend to talk about everything in terms of stress. If we're having the kind of day that we'd rather forget, we may say that we're "stressed out." We talk about being "under stress," or in a period of "intense stress," or we may say that we're in a "high stress" job, or that life in general is "too stressful."

Although we use this word today, in years past we might have said that we were pressured or concerned or worried, or we could have said that we were carrying many burdens. Call it what you will, but the reference we keep making is, in more simple terms, to life itself. Sure, some lifestyles and jobs are more stressful than others. But is the doctor on a typical day any more or less stressed than the teacher at final exam time? Is the mechanic under pressure any less stressed than the unemployed person searching daily for a means of income?

The reality is, we are all under stress, regardless of our station in life, or the direction we pursue. This is about attitude and how we view our life path.

A Matter of Attitude

How we feel about what is going on in our lives has much to do with our expectations, our attitudes, and our beliefs. It probably also has much to do with our basic constitution—the hand we were dealt at our birth—and our personality. We all know people who seem to thrive on pressure. They have always amazed us, haven't they? Perhaps *their* control stresses *us* out! Imagine someone who likes nothing more than a challenge and a deadline. At one time, anyone who was like this was labeled as a "Type A" personality, but over the years, researchers have recognized that the high-powered personality who enjoys the hectic life is not necessarily headed for heart disease or other illnesses. No, a high-powered label doesn't automatically mean that the person is hostile or volatile, as has been suggested before.

I suspect that these personality types thrive on pressure no matter where they live or work. After all, many of these people would not call what they experience stress. Many would say that they are living up to their potential, or they would talk about their ambitions, or they might say that they like situations that demand total concentration.

In other words, what is stressful for one person may be sought out or desired by others. Much of what happens to us happens to just about everyone in our busy, hectic society. How we react to it is up to us—on some days, our reactions to events may be the only thing we can truly control. Over time, when we use quality thinking to change our lives, we may make conscious decisions to implement plans that make us more comfortable with ourselves and our activities. Some people may seek to reduce stress, and others do not even see themselves as being in a state of stress; the evaluation is subjective. The reality is that many of us simply make trade-offs among the kinds of pressure we like and don't like.

For example, Ben has a three hour commute every work day. Most of his friends can't understand how he takes it day in and day out. But Ben has a routine. He listens to books on tape in his car, or some mornings he tunes in a radio call-in show, and often, on the way home he plays classical music that he enjoys. Ben frequently finds himself in traffic jams, but they don't bother him. A few minutes saved or lost either way don't matter that much. By the time he gets home, his long commute has given him "down time" between his work life and his family. "By the time I'm with my family again," Ben says, "I've left work problems behind and I'm ready to interact with them in a relaxed and engaged way. The drive home actually invigorates me. Of course, I never go into the city on weekends. I'm a suburbanite for those two days. On some weekends, I never even get into my car."

Is Ben a saint? I mean, could you see *yourself* living that way? Frankly, I couldn't handle that kind of commute. I like the convenience of the city and the transportation services that are available every minute of the day. But to Ben, the commute is part of the decision about the most desirable way to live; he and his family have worked out a solution that makes them happy. Ben is not without options. His adjustment to the commute isn't a matter of simple resignation. For example, Ben and his wife, Georgia, annually reevaluate their decision about where to work—and live. They ask themselves if they should:

- Move closer to the city to shorten the commute.
- Consider the idea that Ben should look for a job in a nearby suburb. (Ben's wife, Georgia, has a job in the town in which they live. Her commute is ten minutes.)
- Move even farther away from a city and open a retail store. (This has been a long-term goal for Ben and Georgia for some time.)
- Move into a residential area in the city.

- Rearrange Ben's work schedule so that he can take the train into the city.

When looking at each option, Ben and Georgia can anticipate the stress trade-offs. Because they consider themselves essentially small town or country people, they always reject the idea of moving into the city. Ben says it makes his stomach tighten just to think about it. Moving closer to Ben's job would mean a longer commute for Georgia or the option of her looking for a new position. She enjoys her job and doesn't want to change. In addition, her office is a few minutes away from their children's school and she is able to handle emergencies as they come up. These options are all considered with the big "quality of life" issues in mind.

This couple isn't ready to open a business yet, but they always keep the option open, because they want to keep that goal alive in their minds. The one option they seriously consider is the idea that Ben should take the train to work. They have tried that, but the downtown train station is a long way from Ben's office. Most important, Ben has become accustomed to the long commute and when all factors are considered, it is the least stressful option for everyone concerned.

Without having to think about it very long, I would make a different choice. I'm a city person and would choose to live as close as possible to my job. If I loved my town that much, I'd look for a different job. The commute would be very stressful for me. I suspect that it would be stressful for others as well. In fact, when I hear about people who live with these long traveling hours, I wonder if they have ever considered the notion that they truly do have options. Many people seem to believe they are stuck with the "low quality" solution that has now become habit.

The point here is not to decide what is stressful for other people, but to consider what is stressful for you. I use the example of the long commute because it is a common situation. However, take a look at whatever you believe is adding stress to your life and use your decision-making skills to evaluate what you can do about it.

What are your options? Which option is the best? How can you implement the selected action? And always keep in mind, that it is rarely the specifics of the situation you find yourself in that causes anxiety or fear; it is your attitude about it.

Good Stress / Bad Stress

When the famous Hans Selye conducted his research about stress, he first discussed physical stress. He measured the physical response of rats to cold, heat, being forced to swim in cold water, and so forth. We know that the body has a hormonal stress response—one that is built in and is extremely beneficial to us. Our ability to fight or flee is part of our evolutionary development, and rather than condemn it or worry about it, we should be glad we have it.

If we didn't have physical responses to internal or external stimuli, we wouldn't have this wonderful system of being able to sense our reactions to things. We would lack important data upon which to make decisions about our lives. For example, if Mary has a pounding heart, sweaty palms, and a hostile attitude when she runs into delays on the highway, she knows this is a stressful situation—for her. Mary, unlike Ben, might decide to make changes in her life that eliminate this daily source of stress. She could, of course, change her attitude toward it too. Either option is valid. But, her own stress response system alerts her to her reactions. That's why it is valuable. Just think of the peril we would regularly put ourselves in, both physically and mentally, if we didn't experience our body's natural responses.

I once spoke to a group of professionals whose work load made it necessary to work long hours—sometimes logging even 16- and 18-hour days. Invariably, fatigue set in at some point, and many of them

179

complained about it. They wished they could keep on working without loss of concentration, hunger, need for sleep, and so on, intruding into their days and nights. "Bless that fatigue, don't curse it," I said. "It is a great gift. It's protecting you, keeping you from killing yourself." When looked at that way, it's strange how the perspective about this "stress" changed. We can view the fatigue and the symptoms that go with it as bad stress, but that takes the narrow view.

In fact, whenever you are feeling stressed, take a moment to identify where in your body you sense it, and begin to think about what message that stress is trying to give you. Really! Take a moment to look inside yourself, and establish communication with the part of you that is causing the strain on your body. Ask that part of you what it is after, what positive intent it has by sending you a message. You should not be surprised to have that "sense" send you an answer.

In many cases, you will come to recognize that the part is trying to tell you something quite positive and worthwhile. Some people recognize that the signs of stress are saying: "Slow down so you can concentrate on the task," or, "You're taking on too much at one time and you're harming yourself. Sort it out." In other words, the stresses we experience in our body have a positive intent for us; we just need to take a moment to uncover what that purpose is. The answer is inside for the asking. In this sense, all stress is valuable because it always has a positive message for us.

Traditionally, good stress, technically known as "eustress," is the stress that comes from activities we welcome. For example, if we choose to run a marathon, our bodies will experience stress, but we know we will recover quickly. If we were forced to flee our homes and run this same distance, even the trained runner would have a different attitude about it. Many of the things we consider the most important and valuable parts of our lives bring stress—they must,

because we are alive. If we don't experience any stress, then we are no longer counted among the living.

We can choose to look at all our activities as adding quality and knowledge to our being, even those things we call stressful. We need to take a moment to find out and clarify what the messages of stress are at the time. Are you beginning to see the importance that our attitudes about stress have in the way we permit it to affect us? As we've seen, for Ben, the highway is manageable and even pleasant. For Mary, it is a stressful place. If Mary took a moment to look inside and ask that part of her creating the stress what its positive intent is, she may find the answer emerging: "Because you aren't allotting enough time at the office to complete your work." or, "You need more rest and perhaps you can arrange to come into work a bit later, or go to bed a bit earlier, so that you can get the rest you need." In both cases, the stress is part of the life lived. And in both cases, there are options—for the asking.

What We Can Control and What We Can't

In the best of all possible worlds, we chart our own course. But, as we all know, we don't always live in the ideal world. Sometimes, there are factors that are simply out of our control. So, what do we do then? Sometimes we have no choice but to accept what is. Our best friend or lover is seriously ill or a parent has died. We lose jobs and must look for another or the fire in the building next door has damaged our home. Of course, we will feel a range of emotions over these events—sad, angry, resentful, worried, and so on. These are natural emotional responses to life events, informing us of the significance an event has for us.

Too often, people try to fight what are quite natural responses. It's as if feeling bad about something is a curse to be avoided. But much

181

energy is displaced when we try to deny or rise above our emotional responses. Furthermore, denying our experience prolongs the period before we come to acceptance.

One of our biggest challenges in life is discerning what we can change and what we can't. The famous Serenity Prayer (God, grant me the serenity to accept the things I cannot change, the courage to change the things I can, and the wisdom to know the difference) is widely known because it directly addresses this universal human predicament. When we seek to create a quality life, we face this challenge constantly.

Furthermore, because life is very complex, and in our modern society we have so many options to choose among, we will also consider what we can change *now*, versus what must be delayed. In other words, we may have to accept less than optimal choices in some areas, but only for now. In other situations, we may have to come to permanent acceptance. The ability to discern, consider, evaluate, choose a path, get off a path, and evaluate the consequences of all our choices are great human challenges. These challenges will bring with them a degree of stress. But, rather than cursing the stress, we learn to look inside and gain an understanding of its positive intent. This makes accepting stress a natural part of being alive.

Taking Care of Ourselves

There are so many stress management books and tapes and seminars around that I won't belabor the topic any further. However, I do urge you to consider the idea of stress and see if you are taking good care of yourself—physically, emotionally, mentally, and spiritually. Go through the following checklist and see if you are living sensibly—you don't need others to tell you how to do that. Within each of us is a place where we know what is wise for us and what isn't—and what is wise usually adds quality. Pay attention to how each of these factors triggers that internal place in you. This will help you make some sense out of your stress level.

- Do you eat regular meals at regular times and are you making good food choices? You probably know what they are; be honest with yourself. If you need help, why not see a nutritionist or other medical practitioner to get some advice? Asking for the service you need to maintain your health is one of the greatest ways to bring quality into your life.

- Are you sleeping well and are you sleeping adequate hours? Raymond, a friend of mine who was interested in quality concepts, realized that he couldn't make desired changes in his life until he dealt with his sleep disorder. His first quality goal was to seek help at a nearby sleep disorder clinic. Marcia didn't have a sleep disorder, but she was tired all the time because she stayed up much later than was good for her. Her mornings were an endless fight to get out of bed and ingest that first cup of coffee. The stress on her body and mind was obvious. A personal quality program wouldn't be worth the cost of this book if she didn't deal with that. These are extreme examples, but evaluate the way you are scheduling your days and make sure you are feeling as well as you can.

- Do you make time for your favorite people? For some, this means family members; for others, this means friends. When was the last time you talked to your best friend? Have you been too busy to call the sister you miss? Are you happy with this level of quality, or do you want to make a change? Remember, when you deprive yourself of the companionship of people you love, you aren't taking very good care of yourself. Your social needs and the need for emotional intimacy are as important as your need for satisfying work.

- Do you have a quiet period every day for reflection, meditation, prayer, journal writing, or some other activity that puts you in touch with yourself? I recommend that this time be taken in addition to the time you spend planning, goal setting, and organizing lists of what you want to do. The quiet time you spend helps you know yourself better, and therefore serves to guide you in the direction you want to go. Consider the planning sessions the time that you integrate your vision and desires with your goals and plans. As quality concepts become more and more a part of your life, you will see more harmony and balance—what you want and what you actually do will begin to look and feel the same.

- Do you take care of your body, or do you treat it as if it is your servant? Many of us view our bodies as workhorses and we are shocked when they rebel. In addition to adequate nutrition and rest, we also need adequate activity. You don't need me to tell you that you should have a regular exercise program—you already know that. So, what are you doing about it? Are you trying to bring quality into your life without a quality body? Does this make sense? If you haven't done well in this area, then consider making a change.

- Do you renew your spirit on a regular basis? For some people, community or religious activities are renewing; others paint, draw, or play music to revive their inner spirit; still others seek time in nature or they work in a backyard garden. If you have filled your life with activities that deplete rather than renew, then bringing quality to your life isn't going to be easy, is it? You may not be able to make a change all at once, but consider this need for life-giving renewal. It's one of the best stress management techniques you'll ever hear about.

- Do you experience stretches of boredom? Some experts believe that being bored is one of the most stressful situations we can

possibly create. If you find yourself bored, then consider why this might be. Why has the zest left your life? What can you do to remedy this situation? Does boredom have a place in your vision? When I hear a person talk about being bored, then I'm usually talking to a person who has no vision.

The Answers Are Within

For now, realize that stress is simply a part of life. Learn to take a moment when stress is sensed and look inside yourself. Ask "what is your positive intent for me?" and permit the answers to emerge from within. Give them a chance and they will. Your unconscious mind will send you a message about what it is concerned about. The answer always leads to greater awareness, understanding, and positive growth. Ultimately, it adds quality to your life. And isn't that where we started—giving and receiving quality to and from yourself and others? When you evaluate what you want to do with your life today, tomorrow and next year, remember that the answers are within you. The fact is, most of us already know this, and when we need help, it is often to assist us in the process of searching for the best solutions for our own personal situations.

Time Management

Given enough time, there is little we can't accomplish and few problems we can't solve. That's what we have been led to believe. But in so many ways, time is an elusive concept. Nowadays, those who conduct research into time management often comment that people tend to view the hours of the day as absolute—something imposed on them by the outside world. This is not so far from true. After all, we live in a society that runs by clocks, schedules, divisions of the day down to minutes. Our watches tell us how many seconds of a minute have passed. (Except when you're taking your heart rate after exercising, is there ever a time that you really need to know the time in increments of seconds?)

Yet, so many of us believe that we are slaves to this thing called time. We never have enough of it, and we feel pressured by it. We may even buy specific items that promise to save us time. Well, some of these products do save time and some don't. For many people, the search for the next saved minute subtracts quality rather than adding it.

Putting Time in its Proper Place

Human beings have not always lived with clocks and watches, minutes and seconds. As hard as it is to believe, there are still places in the world where people live by sunrise and sunset. They eat when they are hungry. They work until a job is finished or until they are tired or hungry or the sunlight disappears. Some languages do not have words for concepts we take for granted—appointment, schedule, on time, late, early, and so on. Imagine living in an era or a culture when the idea of being "rushed" didn't even exist. Most of us can't imagine living by seasons or pacing our days according to the sun. And, it isn't likely that many of us will ever be able to experience life in this way. Many people wouldn't want to.

A person in my audience once remarked that these other people who lacked all the time-related words in their language must not have much to do, or, perhaps they were a lazy bunch and certainly not interested in quality. Another person in the audience quipped, "Sure, they were lazy as they worked every day just to survive." When we look to the past, let's remember that daily survival for most of our ancestors was a far bigger issue than it is today. We can't say that we need more time in our modern world simply because it takes more work to survive. That simply isn't true.

Being Rushed is No Accident

Ralph Keyes, author of *Timelock: How Life Got So Hectic and What You Can Do About It,* traces the shift in history when time began to be carefully measured and even more important, assigned a monetary value. In previous eras, life's tasks were seasonal and work was defined as the necessary activity to meet human needs. During the industrial revolution people began to be paid by the hour, and a person's time began to be measured in terms of worth. Once time became linked with actual monetary figures, the whole picture changed.

We are living in this rushed manner in part because we say, "time is money." If we work harder, we conclude that we'll make more money. Now, we all know on some level, that this isn't necessarily true, but the pace has been established because time is seen as a commodity we trade. Once time became measured with precision, we could add the concept of schedules and appointments and we began to worry about being late, and the related concept of early was important too.

Late is bad, early is good. But, too early means that we might waste time. What do we do with these valuable minutes that could be spent in some "constructive" way? Remember now, this is recent thinking. Most human beings have lived and died without worrying about wasting time.

It follows that if we begin to view time as money, then we can spend it in a variety of ways. Most of us have absorbed the idea that work is when we make money, and leisure is when get to use the rewards of the money. It isn't too big a leap in attitude to begin to view anything that is fun as not quite as valuable as the time we spend working for money. Even work took on a negative concept.

Work as play? Why, that's for children. Our work for money concept fit well into the beliefs of our Puritan ancestors that idleness is sinful.

I can't count the number of people I know who look at the hours they spend earning money as time better spent than the hours they spend on the golf course or at the movie theater. Theoretically they know that they need leisure time and they need time with family and friends, but many people feel guilty about it. Some believe that they are "goofing off" when they aren't trying to make money—translated as working. However, quality mind–quality life thinking can serve to redefine those patterns.

In our complex society, there is no way that we can avoid the concept of time as money. It is a fact of life and I'm not suggesting that we do away with it. Money is the primary means of exchange in our culture, and we aren't going to go back to the land-based economy, which, after all, still required some money. What Keyes points out in his book, however, is that we can try to change our attitudes about time, and we can look at our lives as far more than a race against the clock. What he proposes in his valuable book is that we rebel a bit against the more-is-better, faster-is-better, mentality that adds stress and tension to our day-to-day activities.

Time Savers or Time Traps

Once time began to be measured out in seconds, minutes, and hours, with each increment assigned an intrinsic value, then the notion of wasting time arrived. Furthermore, if we can waste time, we can also conserve or save it. Ralph Keyes examines the kinds of time savers we are bombarded with on a daily basis and asks us to consider if they are really time savers, or could they be time traps, which actually rob us of quality.

The average household nowadays has an array of gadgets, appliances, and procedures designed to save time. Microwaves are commonplace—meals in minutes. Washing machines, with dozens of choices of settings, have replaced hand washing and wash boards. Telephones save us the time of writing letters or even the time of going to see our friends or family. Food processors save the time of chopping and shredding, VCRs save us the time of going out to movies, and cash cards save us a trip to the bank.

However, consider what some of the time savers have actually brought. As we all know, progress always comes with a price. Microwaves may save us time, but is the family dinner hour becoming a thing of the past? Members of a family I know take turns making a microwave dinner every night, and then they each carry it off to their own space within their house. With three television sets, they all have different preferences, and the mother in the family would rather read a book than watch the news or a sitcom. Actually, she'd rather sit with her whole family, but they wander off after the six minute dinner is made. (She has succumbed to this routine, because with her full time job and no one willing to share cooking and other family chores, she would be stuck with all the work of fixing a meal and cleaning it up. She isn't happy about the isolated dinner hour, but it's better than the' resentment she felt before.)

This same family has cable television, allowing more choices and, let's face it, more stress. One of the teenagers in the family can't watch an entire program because he can't keep his fingers off the remote control. The family has a blender that's never used, an elaborate food processor that's never been out of the box, and four phones that can be programmed for automatic dialing, but it took a lot of time to set up the system.

What is particularly interesting about this family is that its members know something is wrong, but they aren't sure just what it is. The husband and wife each has a job that is considered "high-stress" and they are often called at home, and the fax machine might start up at any time. There isn't a clear separation between activities outside their home and activities inside their home that are family-centered. Do all the gadgets and time-savers really add to the quality of their lives?

No one can say what this family should do to bring quality back, but Ralph Keyes suggests that we ask ourselves each time we purchase one more item that promises to save time, if our quality of life will be improved. There are people, for example, who were convinced that their businesses depended on their instant availability and their ability to serve their clients in a moment's notice. So, to that end, they gradually added a car phone, and a fax machine, and they began to routinely bypass regular First Class mail and send everything by FedEx. A man I know was quite surprised one day when a client called him and told him that someone had to be in the office to receive the overnight mail or the Federal Express. He didn't like to feel pressured to be in his office all the time in order to receive all this rushed correspondence. "Let's slow down here," he said. "Most things don't have to be done the day before yesterday."

Most of us would be shocked if our clients expressed this sentiment, but think back to the times that you called when you could have written, faxed when you could have mailed, Express-mailed when First Class mail would have done just as well. Meanwhile, we have to work harder to pay for the increased expense of doing business.

Ralph Keyes does not suggest, and neither do I, that these conveniences are without value. But what he does ask is that we put them in perspective, that we maintain the control over our own sense of priorities. I would add that we need to think about any convenience in terms of the quality it adds to our lives. When we put these issues in the quality framework, then we have another concept to help us make decisions. We can ask ourselves if we're using time doing

things that we don't like and then squeezing in all the enjoyable activities in the remaining few hours of our day or week.

Simplify and Enjoy

Many time management books urge us to simplify our procedures and our tasks in order to save time *and* make our activities more enjoyable. For example, we may decide to forgo a time-saving appliance because we enjoy the process of doing the job the slower way. Or, it might save a parent time to put a children's video in the VCR instead of reading a story to a child. But, is this time-saving activity worth it in the long run? Or, is the act of saving time actually subtracting quality?

Another example might be the tendency most of us have to do more than one thing at once. We listen to the news while we cook dinner and watch it while we eat. We might record a movie while we watch another program, all the while trying to read the newspaper. Then the phone rings and we listen to the message on the machine and decide whether we want to pick up. Meanwhile we have one ear to the television and the paper is still in our hand. What are we trading off when we try to fill each minute with activity? We may be adding stress to our lives, unnecessary stress, and we may be fooling ourselves that we're getting more done just because we're doing so many things at once. We may be subtracting quality, rather than adding it.

At work, you might spend hours figuring out ways to save time, but meanwhile your customers aren't being served because you're trading time for quality. One small business owner spent hours pouring over reports about new health insurance plans that were available to his company. The options were numerous, but when he actually examined them, the differences between five of the eight choices were so minimal that he had pressured himself for nothing.

He could have reviewed the three plans in less than half the time. When he spoke to the insurance consultant about this, she said, "Most customers are displeased if they don't have many options. They think we're cheating them." The business owner quickly responded, "What you did was cheat me out of valuable time. I'd keep it simple."

Let's look for small ways to simplify the way we live as much as possible in order to spend time doing the things we really value. In other words, we can use the best of the time management techniques not solely for the purpose of saving seconds and minutes, but to eliminate the time traps and the even some of the so-called time savers.

Take a look at your life and see if you have fallen into excessive time-saving efforts. What are you gaining by these efforts? Do you experience more or less stress in your life now that you moved into a bigger house? When you added the third car for your teenager, are you better off or are you spending more money and time in maintenance? What conveniences actually take up space and are more complicated than they're worth? When was the last time you said "no" to a request to do something you really didn't want to do? Are you spending busy time with many people instead of relaxed time with a few good friends? Do you feel pressured to fill your evenings with work, work, and more work? Is this work really advancing your career? Are you earning more money, or are you diluting your goals? Did you recently add a time-saving device to your home? Has it saved you time, or did you have to spend valuable hours learning how to use it?

These questions, like others throughout the book, aren't meant to make you feel more pressure or more stress—nor are they meant to make you feel bad about yourself. Most of us have become used to the notion that we're supposed to save time and pack more into every minute. But, we're concerned about quality here, not just quantity. We usually can't learn to speak French and work on a Ph.D. in Computer Science at the same time. When we try to do this, we most likely find that we're out of balance—something doesn't feel right.

Our friends may tell us that we're under too much stress. That may be true, but it is also possible that we simply made some choices that aren't working well for us. We may need to simplify and say, "I'll study French next year. I'll finish my degree first."

As you begin to simplify and bring more quality into your life, you may find that you are part of a trend. Many people in our country are doing the same thing. People have begun to realize that they are not machines, built to do it all, and do it faster and faster. People have also begun to realize that rushing around usually results in stress, but it doesn't necessarily accomplish more or add to a quality life.

Sensible Time Management

When you begin to set goals and make plans, you will want to look at the ways you can slowly change work habits that need improvement. You may also want to look at ways that you can improve efficiency and avoid stress-producing wasted time. Many time management experts have come up with some good ideas that we can use in our personal management programs. Below are some of the tips that have worked for me over the years. Remember that these aren't rules. Try them out and see what works for you.

- Break large projects into small pieces. When you face the task of cleaning an entire five-room apartment, it seems overwhelming, but you will be cleaning one room at a time. One room doesn't seem like such a huge undertaking. It has a manageable beginning and a tangible end. Anyone who has taken on a large project will tell you that dividing up work into manageable parts always makes it easier to begin.

- Eliminate what you don't care about. You are attending a weekly social gathering that no longer interests you. Why? What are you gaining? Simply give it up if it isn't contributing anything to your life. Chances are, if your enthusiasm is gone, you aren't giving much to the group either. You may be attending the event because you are friendly with a few people who are regulars in the group. Perhaps you can arrange to see them at others times and in settings you enjoy more. At work, are you doing a job that you can easily hire someone else to do? Delegating is one of the best ways to reduce stress and save your time for projects where your skills and talents can be better used.

- Try to control the paper flow into your home and office. You aren't obligated to open every piece of mail that comes along. Look at the return marking. Do you care about the organization that is soliciting money? Do you get frequent mailings from them? Why not drop them a postcard and request that you be removed from their list? The other alternative is to continue to throw away mail unopened. Some people find it useful to set aside a regular time every week or so to sort through the accumulated paper. They handle correspondence, filing, bill-paying, and so on, during this one period of time that they set aside for it.

- Develop concentration skills. Turn your answering machine on when you are working and return the calls later. Close the door to your office and have your secretary hold all calls. If you are preparing a report, work on that as if this were the only project in the world. People who accomplish many different things usually are able to focus on each task at hand. Think of everything you do as an opportunity to practice living in the moment. Consider it your "Zen" training. Zen masters often talk about putting full attention on each task at hand—no matter how trivial. For example, if you're talking on the phone, carry on your conversation but don't wash dishes or balance your checkbook at the same time. If you're balancing your checkbook, focus all your attention on that task. You'll work more efficiently, and you'll also be more relaxed when you move to the next job.

Time management is a process. I don't advise trying to change everything all at once. Take each idea and work with it until you are comfortable. When you try to change everything all at once, you end up feeling more pressure, not less.

Getting Organized

Most of us believe, at least somewhere deep inside, that if we could only get organized, we'd set the world on fire. Women in particular have received endless advice about organization, as if a few techniques could make the impossible job of being full-time workers and full-time homemakers possible. (Fortunately, this is changing and many women have given up trying to do everything.) Most people, men and women, eventually learn that if we are attempting to do more than one human being can do, becoming better organized is not going to help.

Let's approach organization from the point of view of quality. If you could organize one segment of your office or home right now, what would it be? How would the quality of your life change if little elves came in and straightened it all out for you? Would your stress level be lowered? Would you save time? Would you enjoy that part of your home or office more? If you can answer yes to all three questions, then I would bet that setting aside a few hours or a whole day to reorganize the space would be worth the time.

In the next month, why not take an inventory of your days, as well as your work and play spaces and decide what you what to change in terms of organization. You may learn some interesting things about yourself. For example, you may learn that an entire area of your house can be eliminated. Sounds impossible? I recently heard about Al, who had resolved for months to clean up his basement workshop. Every weekend the daunting task hung over his head. His wife wasn't pleased with the mess, and he kept procrastinating about projects that he'd planned.

Al had an interesting experience when he began to think about what he really wanted in his life. As it turned out, he really had no desire to put up shelves in the workshop or sort through the many tools he owned. One Saturday morning he told his wife that he was calling a charity and donating all but the most basic tools. But, his wife protested. What about the shelves he was going to put up in the guest bathroom? What about the bookcase he was planning to build? Al's solution was simple. He called a carpenter to put up the shelves and he bought a bookcase. The tools were loaded onto a truck and Al had instant organization. He simplified his problem and reduced stress in his life. He never wanted to become a home handyman anyway.

If Al had really wanted to putter in his basement, he would have taken the time to organize the workshop. It would have added quality to his life. As it turned out, Al had been wasting energy trying to get himself to do something he didn't care about in the first place.

Delegate and Call in the Experts

Some people believe that they must do everything themselves— although I never understood why. If you work in a four-person office and you're the boss, do you end up staying late when everyone else is going home? Do your employees have time on their hands? Why not train other people to do some of your work? If you find your-self uneasy, ask yourself why. It may be that you want to control more than it is practical to control.

You may also find that you are doing unnecessary work. No one can address this issue except you, but do address it. If necessary, invest in an organization specialist to take a look at your office systems. He or she may have many suggestions to help you streamline the way you do things in your office. It may be that your procedures are faulty, not you. All too often, we blame ourselves for not knowing things—as if we *should* be able to do everything and we *should* know everything about our businesses just because we're the owners. Part of being organized, saving time, and reducing stress is knowing when to call in the "troops" to help us. Do you want to be an expert on organizing or do you want to become more organized? An expert may just be able to help you accomplish your goal.

There are organization experts who can help you in your home as well as in your office. You may have to sit down and think about your priorities at home in order to decide what kind of physical organization will serve your needs. Your needs are not the same as any-one else's. A family of six is going to have organizational needs dif-ferent from those of a single person or a two-income family. For some people, optimal organization will mean adding certain tools—a real file cabinet instead of a shoe box full of receipts, for example. For other people, like Al, it might mean eliminating things. Perhaps it's time to clean out the closets and the attic and give away what you don't want or need. It's amazing how "stuff" can add to many people's stress levels.

One-Stop Planning

After we organize our environment we usually want to feel better organized internally. For example, all time management books suggest keeping close track of the daily tasks that we have to do. Obviously, keeping an accurate daily calendar, noting all the jobs we need to do that day is a good way to accomplish this. There are dozens of different systems on the market that can help you do this. Some are computer-based and others are organized in a portfolio. But the important issue is to record your planning all in one place. You should have one daily calendar for business and social appointments, and that same system should allow room for you to make *one* list of all the tasks you need to accomplish that day—no more endless lists that are scattered all over the office, house, and car.

Many years ago, I read a tip about organization, and in the past I've seen it repeated many times. This hint suggests that we make a list of the most important things we have to do that day. We should work on those jobs and not worry about anything else. Then, make a list of tomorrow's most important tasks. If you didn't get the important things done, then start with what's left the next day. Be sensible about the tasks you choose. If you put all the huge tasks on your daily calendar, you are setting yourself up to feel stressed out. Your daily calendar is the place to list the immediate tasks and that same organization system should have appropriate space for long-term planning. Then you can take the small tasks you need to do to accomplish your long term goal and add them when appropriate to your daily task sheet in your organizer.

If you are working to add quality and balance to your life you will probably have a period of time every week or two that you use as a planning session. You'll be assessing your goals and your plans and your weekly or monthly organization tasks. Your daily calendar will grow from these plans—at least in part. Part of your internal organization will be to carefully plan your time and your days in such a way that the quality you want will seem to flow into your life.

You may find, as many people do, that stress is greatly reduced when you make extensive use of organization and time-management systems. After all, you don't have to remember so much if you write tasks down. But remember, calendars can become a tyrant as well as a helper; if we live only by daily task lists, then we may find ourselves being ruled by them. The point here is to find a balance. Decide what is crucial, what is merely important, what is optional if there's time, and what can be eliminated altogether.

Remember Angela, the woman who made the decision to move to a new city, start a business, and establish a new life? She used the decision implementation form to divide the daunting tasks of moving into numerous parts. If she hadn't done this, she would have always wondered what she should be doing, what had she forgotten about, what that nagging task was that she was supposed to be tackling today.

A daily time-management and organization system Angela installed on her computer kept her planning relatively free of stress. In fact, she later told our quality group that she was relaxed throughout the entire move—so relaxed that she thought something might be wrong with the way she was implementing her decision.

It's All of a Piece

I've grouped stress management, time management, and organization together because when we look at them individually, we invariably see where the others fit. Try as we will, we can't separate our attitudes toward time from stress, nor can we avoid stress if we always feel disorganized. Furthermore, we believe we are wasting valuable time when disorganization hits us in the face and then we say we're stressed out.

The goal of personal management is to add quality to your life, and without addressing your attitudes and habits in all three areas, you can't possibly achieve the level of quality you desire. Consider doing the following short exercises to assess your attitudes toward stress, time, and organization:

- If you believe that you don't have time for a new project or plan, take a few minutes and jot down why. Are you afraid of adding more pressure to your life? More stress? Is there something you can eliminate from your life that is not bringing quality into it anyway? If you get rid of the "offender," will you have time for the plan you prefer?

- Are there specific times during the day when you find yourself doing three things at once? What creates the necessity for this? Can you eliminate one of the three? Could you try it for a day or two? What do you think will happen? If you feel fear, ask the fear what it's trying to tell you. You may be surprised at the answer. The fear may be little more than the reaction to the work ethic common in our society—more is better. This message is: If you can do one thing at a time, surely you can do two or three. What would happen if you did each task in succession?

- If you are one those people who rushes all day, find out what you are avoiding? I do mean, avoiding. If we fill our days with endless activities, then we can't stop to make plans, find our vision, set our goals. This approach is designed to reduce stress by facing situations that are eating away at us. As you work with the quality ideas you will find that you experience an inner sense of calm even in the midst of concerns and worries.

Rushing is also one way to avoid difficult relationships or it can be an excuse to avoid facing a health problem. Many a 50-year-old man has "rushed" himself to the emergency room only to be told that he can't work for months. Later, we learn that he hated his job anyway and he used rushing to avoid facing it. "I thought it was my lot in life," one man said. Another thought that if he kept rushing he'd keep his job. But he was a downsizing casualty anyway.

- Look around your home. Is there a job that you know needs to be done and its very existence makes you anxious? Perhaps it's the corner of a room that is overloaded with magazines, junk mail, half-read newspapers, and so forth. You keep meaning to sort it out, but you can't get to it. Why not take a quick glance through to salvage anything really important and then throw out the rest? Instant organization!

Half finished sewing or craft projects, tools that are never used, clothes you've been meaning to alter, wallpaper that needs hanging, mail that isn't answered, and so forth, add to our stress, coax us to believe we don't have enough time, and give us ammunition to berate ourselves with. What are your options?

Even just a minute of thought suggests that you could:

- Call your sister or a friend and find out if she or he wants to finish these craft projects. Or, call a rehab or training center in your community and find out if the projects could be valuable to them. If they don't want them, throw them out.

- Give the tools away to friend or to a charity, after you've saved a few crucial ones. Don't kid yourself; you might be like Al. You never wanted to refinish furniture or build a bookcase anyway.

- Take the clothes to a consignment shop so they can be bought by a person who can wear them, or take them to a tailor next week and get all the alterations done at once.

- Call a handyman service to hire someone to hang the wallpaper. Cut back on expenses somewhere else. Or, clear the calendar and do it next weekend. If you aren't inclined to do that, the wallpaper might sit for another six months.

- Either answer the mail this coming week or throw it out. Or, call the people who have written to you. Chat for a few minutes and consider the job done. If you don't write letters but want to stay in touch, then set aside some time each week or each month to call the people you would like to stay in touch with.

- Every day for one week, make a list of the most important things you have to do that day. I suggested this before as a concept, but now I'm suggesting it as a powerful time and organization management tool. If after a week, you don't find that it brings quality into your days, then drop it.

- For one full day, live as if time and organization didn't matter. Remember, this is the way much of world lived in the past—some people still live this way. Take off your watch and just live moment by moment. Some people find it helpful to unplug the phone and avoid the radio or television during this experiment. You may find yourself slightly uncomfortable, but you can get past this response. Listen to your internal feelings. What are they telling you? You might learn that you have forgotten how to be quiet and to live a moment at a time. Some worries may emerge or you may find yourself thinking about what is missing in your life.

That's great! Congratulations, you have a chance to get back in touch with the "you" that often feels stressed out or bogged down. You may go a long way in identifying your deepest desires. You *can* bring about the kind of quality days you have been longing for over the past several months or even years.

You have learned much about many life skills. Sure, you already had some knowledge, but now your Resource Inventory is richer by far. So, what are you going to do now? In the next chapter, you'll see how you can use all the ideas and concepts presented in this book to bring more quality into your life. And why do you want this increased quality? Chances are, you read this book in the first place because you wanted to change your life in some way. You have the tools to pursue happiness in a systematic and organized way. Now you'll learn how working with quality concepts helped enrich and energize many lives.

CHAPTER IX

And the Pursuit of Happiness

IF YOU'VE READ THIS FAR, you've learned that the pursuit of happiness involves possessing many attitudes and skills. First, you read about vision and then you took time to assess the place you find yourself in right now. If you were to do that exercise now, you would probably find that some new skills have been added to your RI, perhaps some new attitudes as well. Terrific! You're on your way when you give yourself full credit for all you've accomplished and all you already have. You have enhanced your life by learning how important certain skills are to you and the way they allow you to give and receive quality.

Along the way, we've seen Cindy struggle with the issue of vision versus goals; we've watched a young couple from Minnesota reach a compromise that gave them each at least a part of what they needed. We've also seen our friends evaluate their basepoint, the place from which they begin. You've evaluated your own basepoint as well. Perhaps you wondered why this was necessary. I hope that you now understand that every day, as you pursue quality, you are expanding your basepoint and your Resource Inventory. In other words, each day you have a new basepoint and an enlarged RI. Give yourself credit for that.

Gentle Reminders

As we've gained glimpses into the lives of others, I hope that you have related their experiences to your own. If you need a reminder about some of the basic concepts our acquaintances have learned, then go back to Chapter Three and review the material there. Better yet, go back to Chapters One and Two and think about your vision. Perhaps your vision has changed—you may even have a better understanding of what having a vision means.

Like Cindy, you may realize—at last—that you don't start from the proverbial "Square One." No, you start from some square that we won't even bother to number—it would be far too big a number on this group of squares along the path. For many of the people I've worked with in the past few years, this has been an empowering idea. They have looked at their own backyards and have seen the flowers through the weeds. Like many of the people you've met in this book, the backyard may be filled with unpleasant memories and even tragedy. However, your commitment to your own pursuit of happiness through the quality principles is a sure sign that you have resolved to overcome the problems of the past and are determined to move on. Happiness may not be a birthright, but the pursuit of it is. It is your essential right and privilege to examine your backyard and plant the seeds of a new life.

It May Not Be What You Thought

I become excited when I think about the ways in which some of the people I've worked with have learned to use quality mind–quality life ideas to pursue their dreams and goals. Just last month, I checked in with April, a woman who wanted to change everything all at once. In our group, we urged April to slow down and take things one step at a time. It was difficult to put a cap on her energy well, but eventually

April said, "Okay, okay, I'll start with my health and move on from there." In the pursuit of happiness, April couldn't have picked a better area in which to launch her pursuit of happiness—and a quality life. Let's look closely at April's story.

When she decided to work with our group, April was suffering from a disease that some doctors told her was irreversible. Her only choice was to take powerful drugs, which had ominous side effects, for the rest of her life. April was just about to undertake this course of treatment when she "happened" to run into a friend who suggested that she try a non-traditional approach to treating this disease. By the second week of our group session, April had scheduled a visit with this practitioner. Prior to this chance encounter with her friend, April was resigned to a traditional course of treatment, and she was ready to plunge into tackling career and social issues instead. She was, to the best of her abilities, planning to ignore the health concerns—pretend that they didn't exist. Through the gentle nudging of our group (having "quality" buddies really does help) April rethought the issue.

When April looked at her basepoint, she found that the career issues and expanding her social life could both wait. She had a secure job as a manager in a prosperous retail store. Her circle of friends was large, but she believed she had outgrown many of the people. At age 40, she was determined to expand her Resource Inventory, starting with the people in it. We pointed out that April's friend who referred her to a non-traditional healer was a valuable part of her RI. Her job was a valuable resource, too, because it was secure, the salary was adequate—even slightly better than adequate—and she enjoyed going to work each day. (Her goal was to have her own retail consulting business, but she agreed to delay working on this until she had explored her health problems in more depth. She chose exploration over resignation.)

The group also recognized the strength in April's initial impulse to get on with life in spite of her potentially serious problem. This showed a great commitment to bring quality into her life. But, making the choice to explore other treatments also showed that she was attempting to bring even more quality into her life. When she looked at it from that point of view—one of quality, versus acceptance of less than the best that was possible—she quickly saw that she had been selling her life a little short.

In the next months, we heard April's excitement over the new treatment. As it turned out, the condition could be partially improved and controlled with an exercise and diet program, which gave her still more energy with which to go after quality in other areas of her life. April's energy was directed toward her social life, starting with a support group that she started for people who suffered with the same illness. April brought quality to her own life and helped bring quality to those who shared her problem. We had never seen April so excited and focused.

For several months, April pursued this project and her own health began to improve as well, "Every day I must do certain things in order to maintain my level of energy and well-being," she said, "so I don't have a lot of room left for other goals." That was fine—she was taking it a step at a time.

April made many close friends within her support group and when I last spoke to her, she was doing her first consulting job, which had already strengthened her client's business. She still had her day job, but she was gaining some experience that could be put to use when and if she decided to leave her position and do the consulting work full time. April's approach to this pointed out how much quality decisions can be subjective.

During the period of time in which April had to concentrate on her health, her longing for a business was put on hold. April told the group that it wouldn't have brought quality into her life to quit and be without a secure income while she was undergoing expensive treatment. In other words, in April's case, quality meant hanging on to some aspects of the status quo. Perhaps this will happen to you as well.

As you pursue a personal quality program, you will pick and choose among many areas in your life. You may retain the level of quality you already have, because to do otherwise might lower the quality of other parts of your life. Later, when the time is right, you can make the change you want. It's all a matter of balance.

April's story also points out that we can make some changes gradually—the pursuit of happiness doesn't mean, as we've said before, that we chuck everything.

April's job was an important component of her Resource Inventory, one she could use to her advantage as she worked on other things. This story also points out that we can "dabble," if you will, in our dreams. What if April had quit her job and attempted to establish a consulting practice only to find out that she didn't like it? By doing some moonlighting, April is testing the waters. She has an escape hatch to use if she doesn't like the dream after all. This is one of the most important lessons of personal management and its use in the pursuit of happiness. If anyone tells you that in order to change your life you must find one dream and pursue that dream for all time, then you should quickly review the quality principles. Dreams will change, opportunity will look different today than it did yesterday, you will be a different person tomorrow, and like April, you may change your goals and dream new dreams.

In April's case, the work with the support group was so satisfying that she chose to be a consultant on a very part-time basis. In fact, April found that she was expanding in so many areas because of this support group activity that she entertained the possibility that she would change career direction completely. "I might want to work with a foundation that studies this illness," she said, "and get out of the retail business altogether. We'll see."

Our group saw that April's vision was changing too. At first, she articulated her vision as one of teaching others to succeed in a particular kind of work—service work. Now, she seemed to be shifting her vision to improving others' experience of limitation and living with illness. She even began a newsletter that focused on helping others live their lives more fully in spite of illness. When we asked April what area seemed to be benefitting her the most, she said, "As my health improved, I learned spiritual lessons. I learned that reaching out to others is the most important mission I have. Retail work is valuable, and I still love it, but helping others improve the quality of their health and therefore, their lives, has turned out to be the most valuable of the quality lessons I learned."

I use April as an example because she teaches us all that change may come in ways that we never thought about before. April had viewed dealing with her illness as a chore that the group had talked her into (although not in a negative way). She thought of it as something to tackle and get out of the way so that she could get on with other things. But, as it turned out, the work she did on her health concerns led to many wonderful explorations and significant changes in attitude and belief. Of course it also provided a rich source of new friendships. None of this could be anticipated, yet it all happened and unfolded for April in a very exciting way.

I consider April a role model for us all as we put quality mind–quality life concepts into action. Actually, we could ask: If April can live so fully and happily, what's holding us back? Why aren't we starting this program today, even if our first step is small—thinking about our vision, negotiating even one small improvement in our home-life, organizing one corner of the office, or calling one person who has information we need to complete an important project.

Perhaps, as we open up our minds and hearts to quality, we'll have a "chance" encounter with the very person who can help us on our path to happiness. I put the word "chance" in quotes here, because the supposedly accidental or coincidental may not be such. It's possible that we have all kinds of lucky situations present themselves or beneficial incidents occur, but we don't notice them if we're not consciously paying attention. Many people believe that once we are open to them we see these little miracles every day. I know that April became a believer very quickly.

No More Failures

One of your biggest challenges is to change your thinking about the issues we often lump together as "pass and fail." You missed your exercise class two mornings in a row—oh dear, a failure. That's what you usually think, and it may take a lot longer than the time it took you to read this book to overcome this mind-set. You missed your class, and you didn't bring the quality you intended into your life. It's that simple. You have another chance tomorrow. Remember Jim? He was the man in Chapter Four, who was trying to write novels, meet new women, go to graduate school, and find a new home—all in the same day (well almost).

We saw that Jim had set himself up to *not* reach any goals—he calls it failure, but we know better now, and so does he. If you related to Jim's story, then reevaluate now. Are you still stuck in the mold that tells you that you must accomplish the impossible and you are a failure if you don't? Okay, you at least know that you can change this if you want to. It may be one of your biggest challenges as you bring balance and quality into your life. Jim still finds that he slips back into the mind-set that he isn't doing enough. Like many people, Jim feels a bit guilty if he isn't doing something that represents obvious self-improvement. He's working on this now. For Jim, quality and happiness mean that he needs less pressure, not more.

Other people may find that they must encourage themselves to get out of certain ruts. This is the group for whom decision-making becomes a powerful tool. I've found that people who complain about being in a grind or rut, or who are bored, are generally those people who haven't learned to make effective decisions. They keep the same job, because they don't know how to evaluate what they really want. Too many choices seem to loom, and they don't know how to examine all possibilities and eliminate some choices and focus on others. These people aren't failures; they're successfully avoiding change. They're successes at what they are doing at the moment! Sure, they can alter their course, just the way we've seen the super-star businesses do in this country, but they aren't failures. If you find yourself fitting the profile of one who is bored or in a rut, then perhaps you'll want to study the material in the chapter about decisions. Perhaps you'll devote most of your quality mind work to making new choices—one at a time.

If you remember, Angela was very good at not making choices. In fact, she had avoided making decisions so well that life just drifted along. She lost a relationship and a job because she didn't make different choices. We watched Angela as she made many decisions that changed the course of her life. She moved to a new town, pursued part-time jobs, and eventually started a business. These were the big decisions, the result of many small ones.

If you find yourself in a dilemma that challenges every area of your life—as Angela found herself in—then you may want to make the list of choices that Angela did, using the forms I've provided. You may find that your most important tool is brainstorming, that is, noting all the options you have and then choosing among them only after you have examined them all. For your individual pursuit of happiness, the brainstorming technique may be the one most valuable addition to your rapidly expanding Resource Inventory.

Angela was an inspiration to the group with which she was working. She had lived for a long time steeped in a pattern of indecisiveness. She had only the vaguest desires and a bare hint of goals. She wanted to be happy, to have what she called "peace of mind," but she had a difficult time defining what that meant. Mainly, that difficulty came from lack of specifics, not lack of desire for it. In other words, Angela needed to define what these vague concepts of happiness and peace and satisfaction meant to her. Did happiness mean having work that she looked forward to every day? Did peace of mind mean having enough money to live comfortably, but simply, in a new environment? Did satisfaction mean having a sense of being in control of her destiny? In Angela's case, we could answer yes to all three questions. But what about you?

If you're having trouble making decisions, perhaps you should examine some definitions you've been operating with in life. I've found that most people are able to pursue happiness far easier if they understand what that means. This sounds logical and simple, but it's amazing how little training we've really had in this area. Personal management provides the training ground, and it can work for you as it did for Angela and others.

Your first challenge may be to stop drifting along in a particular area of life. By doing so, you may find that everything changes, sometimes quite dramatically—at other times more subtly. Angela drifted along in a bad relationship and one day the man just left. This was a dramatic shift in her life. Over time, she realized that he had done her a favor by leaving. If he hadn't taken the initiative, she would have continued drifting along. You might notice situations in your life that have all the footprints of drifting into mediocrity. I urge you to pick one of those areas and begin to look at all your options. Remember, people on a drifting life-raft may end up somewhere, but it's rarely the place they set out to go. The word "drifting" itself implies that no destination is in sight—or even in mind. Your move toward quality can be the way in which you discover a destination and begin a journey toward it.

Listening and Talking

If you remember, quality thinking involves demanding quality from others; it means not accepting mediocrity or just getting by. To that end, we talked about communications—sending and receiving messages. We learned that there are ways we can improve communication right now, without any special training or fancy techniques. We can eliminate the "global" words, those words that don't communicate specific concerns—always, never, and the universal "they." We learned that we may communicate with our Uncle Jack differently from the way in which we discuss issues with our spouse or lover. We also found that being a good listener may improve communication in one big leap. Bringing quality into our lives may be as simple as listening to the messages that our boss or child or cousin is trying to communicate. Sure, it may not represent the whole quality life picture, but it may be the place that you can begin today.

Steve, a close friend of mine, noticed an immediate improvement in his family relationships because he resolved to talk less and listen more. He sought common ground with his parents and sister, Lacey. They began to respond to him in a more positive way—bringing quality into his daily interactions. This became his first "quality" talk—after he established his vision, of course.

On the other hand, our friend Mark was already an excellent listener, but he resolved to study the philosophy, if you will, of language in order to discover how he could better express himself. Mark also needed to realize that he knew more than he thought he knew—how's that for an exercise in quality mind orientation? Mark uncovered his communication skill strength and improved those areas he believed were holding him back. You might find, now that we're nearing the end of this particular road, that you need to go back to study the communication chapter. Did you skip it or only glance at it, because it seemed to be a tough topic to tackle? Maybe now, when you decide to pursue a quality life, you can go back and look at that material more carefully.

Doing Deals

Every day you are making deals, so to speak. You are negotiating your way around life, and bringing quality into it if you know how to use this skill. We saw Richard bring quality into his life when he learned the elements of successful negotiating. He received a raise and had a great boost in self-confidence because he had done the necessary homework to make his negotiations potentially successful. Although a quality life is not about competing with others to get more and have more, Richard found that learning to negotiate did eventually give him an edge on his job when the next round of promotions and raises came up.

Right now, plan for the negotiating you are going to be doing this week. You may not be able to think of any "deal" you're working on right now, but remember, this skill surrounds just about everything we do. Whenever you believe that the quality you deserve is lacking, that is a time when negotiating may be in order. If this is an area in which you experience a sense of reluctance and inadequacy, then go back and study further. Your quality mind depends on the quality of your Resource Inventory, and improving your negotiation skills may be where you need to begin. Others might be highly skilled in this area, but they need to improve their specific definitions about what they want. While she didn't know it at first, Angela was a skilled negotiator, but she just didn't have a clear grasp about what she needed to negotiate about. So, the skill without the vision or a goal didn't bring the quality of life Angela could have had. And, as we saw, she corrected her drifting patterns and then was able to use the vast skills she possessed.

Variety is the Spice

You are unique and you will pursue happiness in a way that is entirely different from the way your next door neighbor or your co-worker will pursue his or her idea of happiness. And that's what makes the quality philosophy so exciting. You have synthesized the best information from two major worlds, business and self-help, and now you are on your way to making this "marriage" work. This is one of the best partnerships you'll ever have available to you.

The gift of the quality philosophy is best seen in its variety. Yes, the variety of ways you can use it and the variety it will bring into your life. As you have seen throughout this book, individuals have instituted great changes by using this rich but easy-to-begin program. People have changed their lives in positive ways simply by focusing attention on areas in which they wanted to bring in more quality. They accomplish this one step at a time. You can do this too.

Here's an additional sampling of the kinds of changes that were accomplished—sometimes quickly, sometimes slowly—through the power of quality mind–quality life thinking.

- Shelly negotiated a new schedule at work, enabling her to work at home three days a week. (She wanted to do this in order to cut down on her commuting time and be closer to her school-age children.)

- Craig reestablished relationships with his family that had been dormant and empty for nearly two decades. He started creating a quality mind by improving communication techniques, which led to breaking down some long-standing barriers.

- Byron was overwhelmed when he started his personal quality program, so he began by doing a few simple things to reduce stress in his life. He knew what he was about, which involved dedicating his time to working with young people. But, Byron had a full-time job and a big problem with managing his time. Everything else suffered as a consequence and he ended up feeling out of control most of the time. Byron's solution was truly unique in some ways. He took an early retirement, moved closer to the place where he volunteered his time, and resolved to live on less money. Fortunately, Byron's retirement plan allowed him to live at a comfortable if reduced standard of living. His solution probably wouldn't work for everyone, but after reviewing all his options this was the solution that appealed the most.

- Bob left his marriage, which had been a mismatch from the start. He had drifted along for years, never happy, but never doing anything about it. His decision was one based on quality, both for himself and ultimately, for his former wife. His situation shows that quality sometimes comes with some temporary hardship and pain. Change isn't always easy or approved of by others. Bob's mother and sister were furious that he left his wife, calling him irresponsible and selfish. He knew better, and it was months before he was able to smooth out the wrinkles that had formed in his relationship with his family.

- Cathy began an exciting new career in art and design after realizing that her technical job was stifling her creativity. Her decision involved pursuing special courses and spending some weekends and evenings working toward her goals. She had to bring quality into her life by eliminating activities that took too much time away from pursuing her ultimate happiness. Some choices were tough, but necessary.

• David changed his law practice to focus on family law rather than real estate. This may sound like a simple choice, but it involved making some major changes in his marketing and referral system. He had to rethink how he wanted to spend his time and what kind of work gave him the most satisfaction.

• Terry and Pat started their quality program together by signing up for exercise classes at a gym and entering a commercial weight loss program. They realized that nothing was going to help the quality of their relationship more than dealing with health problems that had become serious. (Others have faced up to some serious addiction problems or emotional difficulty that had held them back. Quality simply has no room to enter when a major problem stands in the way.)

• Marcia brought more quality into her life by doing more of what she *wanted* to do and less of what she'd been trained to think she *had* to do. You've probably met people like Marcia—you may even recognize yourself in her. She had spent years trying to be super-woman, doing everything for others and little for herself. Marcia thought she had to cook every day, pursue her career as an attorney-mediator in a school system, volunteer at the neighborhood clinic, and on and on.

In this case, every skill mentioned in this book was brought into use to make changes. Communication—as in saying "no" to requests for her time became her first priority. She communicated her personal needs to her significant others and negotiated with the clinic to reduce her volunteer hours. She organized her life in a way that allowed more free time for herself. Marcia noticed that a strange thing happened. Aside from her friends feeling a bit hurt that Marcia had, as I put it, "gone on strike," the quality of her life became even better because she was no longer resentful and stressed to the limit.

Marcia serves as an example of what happens when one person makes changes. While the boat may be rocked a little bit—or even a lot—other people usually adjust. The fact that the person who has instituted changes becomes happier, more relaxed, or more focused on an issue is generally enough to rally support from others. As we all know, it's more fun to be around happy people than with those who are at odds with themselves and others.

These examples could go on and on. I've personally witnessed people who make major changes and move forward in their pursuit of personal happiness. I've seen people deal with tragedy in their lives and pasts filled with a sense of inadequacy, and supposed failures. But I've also noticed that many people who don't have serious obstacles might be less motivated than those who have had to strive harder. Perhaps these more fortunate people perceive themselves as too lucky to complain. I'm not sure what the reason is, but I do know that every person I've met had areas of life that needed improvement. Sometimes, it's merely the permission to pursue one's personal truth, one's personal happiness, that is needed. Give yourself that permission now to start your journey to a quality life today.

In the past year or two I've experienced many changes in my own life that are the direct result of my own pursuit of happiness using the quality ideas. My career has, as I've said, taken off in new directions, ones that I chose and worked for. My relationships have improved, and I am learning—at long last—to relax.

I recently took a cruise, a type of vacation that was specifically chosen because it promotes relaxation. And, when I first started working a quality management program I faced up to the fact that I needed more recreation and leisure in my life. Before I left for my cruise I made another appearance on the "Today Show" to discuss the O.J. Simpson case. When the interview was over, host Giselle Fernandez smiled as she said, "Well Paul, I know you're off to take a cruise. It's a well-deserved vacation and we'll see you soon." At that point I realized that the goals I set for my life had merged. My dream of working on national television was now affirmed and I was reminded that I was now going off to get the rest and reward I needed after pursuing an important goal. And I was going a long way toward bringing more balance into my life. That cruise did me a lot of good.

I leave you with words that have helped me along the way. Remember the adage: "Success is a journey, not a destination." In your pursuit of quality, balance, and happiness, may these words inspire you the way they have inspired me.